PHP 7 News & Updates
v7.0 – 7.4

ADAM OMELAK
IGOR POCHYŁY

Table of contents

About the authors

Adam Omelak has been developing applications and websites for the Internet needs for over 11 years, using different languages like PHP, JavaScript, JAVA and ActionScript. In 2011, he graduated and acquired an Internet Computing degree at the University of Wales in Aberystwyth, Great Britain. Two years later at the same university, he completed a title of Masters of Science in Software Engineering, by writing a dissertation based on Zend Framework 1.

An author of "Zend Framework 3: Developer's Guide" - the only English book about ZF3 environment and a Polish version about the same topic. Creator of portals and on-line applications like: Funkcje.net, ZaplanujTransport.pl, GazetkiSklepowe.pl, Polish Shopping List Android and ChangeTires.net with Android app. One of his biggest applications is a web e-learning platform within Frog Education Ltd. made for the education sector in the United Kingdom, Denmark, Australia and Malaysia. The platform is currently used by over 12 million users worldwide.

For two years he worked in London for a company called Portal Technology Ltd. where he created from scratch a new e-commerce application: QuickLive, based on the biggest commercial technology on the market: hybris. He lived in Halifax and worked for Frog Education Ltd. for another 2 years, and he has been working there to the present day (another 4 years) remotely from Wrocław, Poland.

At the moment, he runs his own consultancy company where he designs complex websites based on the latest technologies. He follows new trends and seeks for new solutions, mainly those which are popular in the United States of America. More information about the projects and author's work experience can be found in the following links:

https://www.goldenline.pl/adam-omelak/
https://www.linkedin.com/in/adam-omelak-673134107

Direct email contact: adam.omelak@gmail.com.

Igor Pochyły is a full stack developer with over 10 year experience, using hybrid technology like: PHP, NodeJS or Angular. In 2012 he graduated and acquired a software systems engineer degree at the University of Information Technology and Management "Copernicus" in Wrocław - Poland.

He worked for Getin Bank & LG electronics in the past.Creator of portals like FajneLogo.pl, GdzieKupilas.pl generating millions of views per month.

He currently runs a software company called: IPSoftware.

More information about the projects and author's work experience can be found in the following links:

https://www.goldenline.pl/igor-pochyly/
https://www.linkedin.com/in/igor-pochyły-a07ab7148/

Direct email contact: kontakt@ipsoftware.pl.

Thanks

Adam Omelak:

To my lovely parents, sister and my wife, without whom I would not have written this book. Additionally, I would like to thank the people with whom I was working and from whom I have learnt about PHP concepts, these people are: Steve Holt (Frog Education Ltd. Product Manager), Simon Marshall, Simon Law, and Simon Brahan. At the very end I would like to say a big thanks to Frog Education Ltd., the company for which I still work with, for the opportunity to discover and implement new technologies and solutions during my work on their main application.

Igor Pochyły:

Big thanks to my girlfriend, for her understanding that I did not always have time for her. I hope that after the publication we will have more spare time for together entertainment.

CHAPTER 1.
Introduction

1.1. History of PHP

Before we even touch the new bits and bobs of PHP 7, we should really get to know the beginning of PHP as a whole. This will explain why PHP is a very unusually formed language, why it has some inconsistencies to this day and why it has taken the routes in some unexpected directions in the latest versions.

The creator of PHP is a Danish-Canadian programmer named Rasmus Lerdorf who, being only 28, when he developed the first version of PHP/FI (Personal Home Page/Forms Interpreter) in 1994. The initial version of PHP was a set of Perl scripts used for monitoring on-line users on his website. When the traffic on the page got bigger, he rewrote it into C language along with adding some new features. Soon after that, the currently named PHP Tool source code has been released to the public in 1995. In 1997 PHP/FI 2.0 was released, formerly known as PHP 2, which was then used on over 50 thousands of websites.

```
<!--include /text/header.html-->

<!--getenv HTTP_USER_AGENT-->
<!--ifsubstr $exec_result Mozilla-->
    Hey, you are using Netscape!<p>
<!--endif-->

<!--sql database select * from table where user='$username'-->
```

```
<!--ifless $numentries 1-->
   Sorry, that record does not exist<p>
<!--endif exit-->
   Welcome <!--$user-->!<p>
   You have <!--$index:0--> credits left in your wallet.<p>


<!--include /text/footer.html-->
```

One of the Rasmus Lerdorf's great sayings of was the quote: "I actually hate programming, but I love solving problems". This is why PHP in its initial forms did not follow all technical conventions of other languages like JAVA or C++ but decided to turn more into better usability and quick problems fixing of most websites.

Two more developers joined Rasmus and figured out that PHP/FI has not enough possibilities for the eCommerce applications. They all decided to rewrite the PHP completely from scratch, together with already existing large PHP community. In 1998 they announced PHP 3.0 and cancelled the support of PHP/FI. The new architecture in PHP 3 increased the efficiency and some first objected programming concepts, primarily: modularity and customizations of these modules.

```
<?
include("include/common.inc");
// we do an authentication also here
if (!isset($PHP_AUTH_USER)) {
    Header("WWW-Authenticate: Basic realm=\"$MySiteName\"");
    Header("HTTP/1.0 401 Unauthorized");
    echo "Sorry, you are not authorized to upload files\n";
    exit;
} else {
    if ( !($PHP_AUTH_USER==$MyName && $PHP_AUTH_PW==$MyPassword ) ){
        // if wrong userid/password, force re-authentication
        Header("WWW-Authenticate: Basic realm=\"My Realm\"");
        Header("HTTP/1.0 401 Unauthorized");
        echo "ERROR :  $PHP_AUTH_USER/$PHP_AUTH_PW is invalid.<P>";
        exit;
    }
}
if ( $cancelit ) {
    // when user cancel's I want to go to the front page
    header ( "Location: front_2.php3" );
    exit;
```

```php
        }
        function do_upload () {
            global $userfile, $userfile_size, $userfile_name, $userfile_type;
            global $local_file, $error_msg;
            global $HTTP_REFERER;
            if ( $userfile == "none" ) {
                $error_msg = "You did not specify a file for uploading.";
                return;
            }
            if ( $userfile_size > 2000000 ) {
                $error_msg = "Sorry, your file is too large.";
                return;
            }
            // Wherever you have write permission below...
            $upload_dir = "photos";
            $local_file = "$upload_dir/$userfile_name";
            if ( file_exists ( $local_file ) ) {
                $error_msg = "Sorry, a file with that name already exists";
                return;
            };
            // you can also check the filename/type to decide whether
            // it is a gif, jpeg, mp3 etc...
            rename($userfile, $local_file);
            echo "The file is uploaded<BR>\n";
            echo "<A HREF=\"$HTTP_REFERER\">Go Back</A><BR>\n";
        }
        $title = "Upload File";
        include("include/header.inc");
        if (empty($userfile) || $userfile=="none") {
            // print the form
        ?>
```

The overall syntax looks similar to current version but there were a few main differences. Notice that PHP short tags <? ?> are no longer supported and that every internal constant has a dollar sign before it. Even though PHP 3 started introducing some OO concepts like first internal objects, it was lacking the foundations of classes, inheritances or custom objects. There was only one version of PHP 3 and it was quickly replaced by PHP 4 in just a few months.

PHP 4 on the other hand was a vast improvement to PHP 3; it was completely rewritten from PHP's core engine. A wide variety of new database types and APIs has been added together with better security and efficiency of running more complex applications than just initially personal home pages. Developers quickly started to think out of the box and created e-commerce solutions and Content Management Systems. The PHP engine was finally called Zend Engine as Zend is a combination of first names of creators: Zeev and Andi. Finally support was implemented for multiple HTTP sessions, web servers, buffering and security handling.

PHP 5 is probably the version where we all started learning this language from. It has improved support for OO programming by at last introducing classes, methods, class constants, static methods, inheritance, interfaces and few others. A proper handler of DB was added via PHP Data Objects (PDO) object. There was even an initiative of GoPHP5 provided by PHP developers who were self-promoting move from PHP 4 to 5.

The PHP 6 has never been released, even though it was on the road map. The PHP core dev team did not have enough of the new features and some RFCs have been massively delayed. Hence it was agreed to skip the PHP 6 and release PHP 5.5 instead.

At the moment the latest major PHP version is version 7. There is a lot to say about this major release, but to fully understand the changes and consequences you will have to read this book first :)

1.2. Who should read this book

This book is addressed to experienced developers or at least developers with some basic knowledge of PHP world. This paper assumes that you know what are the OOP, so Object Oriented Principles like: classes, objects, methods or inheritance. There are many PHP books about introduction to PHP language, so there is no reason to repeat their subjects and topics in here. The book is going to start with preferred installation guides of how to run PHP on your own localhost instance instead of using virtual boxes or remote servers. The simplicity of the environment setup is a key we chose to quickly start your journey with the latest PHP changes on your local machine.

1.3. PHP lifecycles

Like any other major language, PHP has separate support dates for feature updates and security patches. Those two are usually close to each other but bug fixing tends to last longer than features. The support dates can vary if the next version is or is not backwards compatible with the previous one.

This book will include any updates if a new semi-major version is announced to the public, so keep checking this document for more updates in the PHP world!

By the beginning of 2019, PHP will only have included support of PHP 7.1 and onwards. This is probably a safe bet to move over to that version before the deadline hits, as too late swap may cause your system being vulnerable to potential bugs and insecurities. The table of all PHP versions from 5.5 to 7.4 is included in the table below.

Version	Initial Release	Active Support	Security Patches
5.5	20th June 2013	21th July 2016	21th July 2016
5.6	28th August 2014	19th January 2017	3rd December 2018
7.0	3rd December 2015	3rd December 2017	3rd December 2018
7.1	1st December 2016	1st December 2018	1st December 2019
7.2	30th November 2017	30th November 2019	30th November 2020
7.3	late 2018	late 2019	late 2019
7.4	early 2019	unknown	unknown

CHAPTER 2.

Installation

2.1. Required applications

In order to start working with PHP 7, we would need a work environment setup and suitable programs. The work environment is a local or remote server that handles services like Apache, PHP, databases and .htaccess. All the things related to the code environment will be outlined in the next subsection of this chapter. Here, however, I will focus on the selection of applications and tools helping to write our code.

Let's start with a basic tool, which is undoubtedly IDE - the programmer's code editor. Every experienced developer for sure knows more than one IDE from among the most popular ones. These are for example: Eclipse, Netbeans, Komodo, Sublime or PHPStorm, which offer support not only for PHP and HTML with CSS, but also for native languages, like JAVA or C++ (of course apart from PHPStorm, which is primarily designed for the PHP development). I have already used all of the above tools and the best choices were: Komodo Edit for very big projects, NetBeans for the smaller ones and PHPStorm for medium size projects. For the purpose of this book and for projects based on PHP 7 I would definitely recommend NetBeans and PHPStorm, most of all due to the native and full support for PHP 7.3 and because it is extremely quick with these projects. My version 8.2 is available to download from the link: *https://netbeans.org/downloads/index.html*, column PHP. If you have a 64-bit version of an operating system, I would recommend you download the Download x64, for any others there is of course a x86 version.

2.2. Setup of work environment

Now, when we have all the required applications, we can begin setting up the work environment, that is the server. To do that we will use a free package called XAMPP, made by Apache Friends. This is a self-configuring set, thanks to which we won't have to do much (apart from the installation) to set it up on Windows machines types. For this book we will be using XMAPP in version 7.2.8, which has the following specifications:

- Apache 2.4.34,

- MariaDB 10.1.34,

- PHP 7.2.8 (VC11 X86 32bit thread safe),

- phpMyAdmin 4.8.2

Bear in mind, that since XAMPP 5.6, Window XP and 2003 are no longer supported. The later versions support only Windows 7 SP1, Windows 8 and Windows 10. Nothing stands in our way to update XAMPP with a more recent version of PHP, like 7.3, this is what we will be doing. We need to first download the PHP codebase from *https://downloads.php.net/~cmb/* and select the most recent version, in our case it's: *php-7.3.0beta2.tar.xz*. We just need to unzip it and paste it into XAMPP root folder and swap the names with existing '*php*' folder (so we can keep the previous version as a backup).

If during the installation process of XAMPP or after running a file from the main folder *xampp-control.exe* and clicking *Start* next to Apache we get an error with the following message:

> The program can't start because api-ms-win-crt-runtime-l1-1.0.dll is missing from your computer

then we would need to install additional C++ libraries: Redistribution package 2008 and Redistribution package 2015. Both of these libraries are available here: *http://www.microsoft.com/en-us/download/↪ details.aspx?id=5582* and *https://www.microsoft.com/pl-pl/download/↪ details.aspx?id=48145* .

After the installation of these C++ libraries we need to open once more the admin panel xampp-control.exe and click the buttons Start next to Apache and MySQL. We should get result shown on the image 2.1.

If we notice an error with the following message:

1:14:33 PM [apache] Possible problem detected!
1:14:33 PM [apache] Port 80 in use by "c:\program files (x86)\skype\phone\skype.exe"!

in such case we would need to go into Skype settings: *Tools/Advanced/Connections* where we can uncheck the option: Use 80 and 443 ports for additional incoming calls.

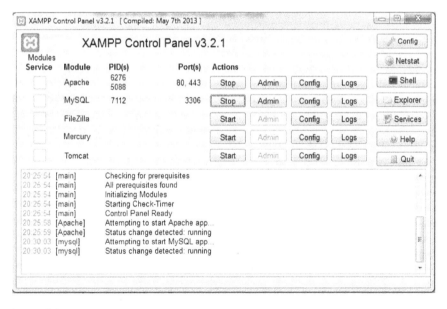

Image 2.1.

For starters we need to double check if our freshly configured server works correctly. We would need to open our web browser and type in: *http://localhost/*. If that doesn't work, then we should try: *http://localhost/xampp/*. The starting page of XAMPP should appear – see image 2.2.

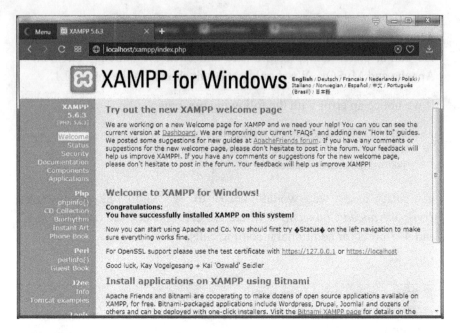

Image 2.2.

The one last check is to verify if our database is also working as expected. To do that we need to click the *phpMyAdmin* link, which should display a list of the available databases and modifications options.

Once we would finally setup our XMAPP instance correctly, we need to install a Composer. It is a tool in the command line, which manages all dependencies of other projects by integrating them with our codebase. The installation of the Composer is done through the command line; the best option is Shell, which is available in the control panel of XAMPP. On the right-hand side there is a Shell button - click it and then navigate to the folder *php/* by typing:

```
cd php/
```

Now we can paste the following code, which will organize the installation on its own (you can copy it from: https://getcomposer.org ↪/download/):

```
php -r "copy('https://getcomposer.org/installer', 'composer-setup.php');"
php -r "if (hash_file('SHA384', 'composer-setup.php') ===
'e115a8dc7871f15d853148a7fbac7da27d6c0030b848d9b3dc09e2a0388afed865e6a3
```

```
d6b3c0fad45c48e2b5fc1196ae')
{ echo 'Installer verified'; } else { echo 'Installer corrupt';
unlink('composer-↪setup.php'); } echo PHP_EOL;"
php composer-setup.php
php -r "unlink('composer-setup.php');"
```

If we get an information complaining about the old version:

```
Composer: Warning: This development build of composer is over 60 days
old. It is recommended to update it by running
"C:\ProgramData\ComposerSetup\bin\composer.phar ↪self-update" to get the latest
version. hp
```

then we are required to type and run:

```
php composer.phar self-update
```

Like you have already noticed, the Composer is available by calling *composer.phar*, which is quite long and unfortunately local. In order to make it easier to use, we need to go to the folder *php/* in XAMPP and create a file in there with the name *composer.bar* with the following contents:

```
@ECHO OFF
php "% ~dp0composer.phar" %*
```

Thanks to the lines above, we can use our new tool without any issues, wherever we are, by simply executing the command composer.

The last thing to finish setting-up the Composer is changing to a development mode:

```
composer development-enable
```

This gives us the option to update all the related dependencies to our local project, even these designed to be injected when in dev mode. In order to verify if our installation was successful, we should type:

```
composer
```

by that we should get a window with contents similar to the following:

```
divix@DIVIX-KOMPUTER d:\RZECZY_ADAMA\_XAMPP\xampp-5.6\htdocs
# php composer.phar -v
```

```
 /////////////////
/Composer/
/////////////////
```

```
Composer version 1.2.0 2016-07-19 01:28:52
Usage:
  command [options] [arguments]

Options:
  -h, --help            Display this help message
  -q, --quiet           Do not output any message
  -V, --version         Display this application version
      --ansi            Force ANSI output
      --no-ansi         Disable ANSI output
  -n, --no-interaction  Do not ask any interactive question
      --profile         Display timing and memory usage information
      --no-plugins      Whether to disable plugins.
  -d, --working-dir=WORKING-DIR  If specified, use the given directory as working directory.
  -v|vv|vvv, --verbose  Increase the verbosity of messages: 1 for normal output, 2

Available commands:
  about         Short information about Composer
  archive       Create an archive of this composer package
  browse        Opens the package's repository URL or homepage in your browser.
  clear-cache   Clears composer's internal package cache.
  clearcache    Clears composer's internal package cache.
```

Image 2.3.

Optionally we can install and setup an application that controls the
version of a code, like GIT or SVN, however this dependency goes
beyond the subjects of this book. Using the version control, we can
safely change the code and go back to the previous versions of the old
code by using the history of changes and logs of these revisions and
branches.

CHAPTER 3.
PHP 7.0

The new version of PHP 7.0 has introduced many additional benefits to the language in terms of new functionality, improved support of existing tools, usage of the most recent algorithms. Also it finally hit a milestone with speed-up performance which finally allows PHP to compete with competitors like: Python or Ruby. For the first time ever PHP has included scalar types and parameters as well as return type declarations.

3.1. New functionality

3.1.1. Scalar type declarations

First and the biggest feature in new PHP version are of course type declarations: `bool`, `float`, `int` and `string` which have been added to the already existing argument types like: `Class/interface` name, `self` or `array`. These scalar types are added to function definitions by prefixing an argument with such type, for instance:

```
function myFunction(string $name, bool $flag) { .. }
```

If we would pass at least one incorrect argument type then we will get a Fatal Error thrown with the appropriate message.

```
myFunction('some_name', 20)
//will result in:
Fatal error: Uncaught TypeError: Argument 2 passed to myFunction() must be an
```

instance of boolean, integer given, called in - on line 1 and defined in -:1

Bear in mind that boolean and integer won't be treated as supported scalar types as they are classes, not types to use in declarations. An alternative for comparing these will be a usage of: `instanceof()`.

3.1.2. Return type declarations

The newly added support for specifying return types for functions are also here. Similarly to the scope of Scalar types, PHP will only support classes, arrays, booleans, integers, floats and strings.

```
function sum($a, $b): int {
    return $a + $b;
}

var_dump(sum(1, 3));
var_dump(sum(1, 3.7));

//will output:
int(4)

Fatal error: Uncaught TypeError: Return value of sum() must be of the type integer,
float returned in - on line 5 in -:5
```

In 7.0 nulls are not acceptable returns types nor are voids available. These bits have been added in 7.1

Both scalar and return type declarations can be turned on and off by strict typing declaration by setting it to 1 or 0.

```
declare(strict_types=1);
```

3.1.3. Arrays in define()

Probably the second most anticipated feature of PHP 7 is an updated `define()` implementation, which now supports any arrays as the values. Since 5.6 we are already able to use arrays in constant definitions so it's a full package now.

```php
class MyClass {
    const TYPES = ['one', 'two";]
}

define('TYPES', ['third', 'fourth']);

//usage
echo MyClass::TYPES[0];
echo TYPES[1];

//will output
one
fourth
```

3.1.4. Anonymous classes

To the anonymous function we now welcome anonymous classes. One of the last most commonly used OO principle is finally here in PHP. We no longer have to create a standard class which then we create and pass into other object, we can now simply create the new class within the method scope to the other object directly.

```php
// Pre PHP 7
class MyClass
{
    public function debug($message)
    {
        echo $message;
    }
}

$util->setDriver(new MyClass());

// From PHP 7
$util->setDriver(new class {
    public function debug($message)
    {
        echo $message;
    }
});
```

As it is just a regular class, you can use extends or implements keywords as you like without any limitation. Classes created in such way are globally accessible.

3.1.5. PHP_INT_MIN

It is a new constant representing the smallest integer for current PHP version. Mostly it's an int of -9223372036854775808 in 64bit systems and -2147483648 in 32bit environments. This constant is usually equal to the reversed `PHP_INT_MAX` which is already available since PHP 5.0.

`PHP_INT_MIN` together with `MAX` can help us identify why a value isn't an integer after checking `is_int()`. This will tell us if the integer is outside of the available inte range or not.

```
function isInteger($input) {
    if (is_int($input)) {
        return true;
    }

    if ($input < PHP_INT_MIN || $input > PHP_INT_MAX) {
        throw new Exception('Input integer is outside of the available PHP range:
'.$input)
    }
    return false;
}
```

The above example will perform a check if the passed argument is in fact a true valid PHP integer value. Otherwise it will examine if the value is just too big or too small; in this case it will throw a new exception with the appropriate message.

3.1.6. Closure::call()

The closure class is a representation of anonymous function in PHP. The first closures can be found in PHP 5.3. The closure in PHP is a callable class to which you have manually bound your parameters. That's the slight difference between closures in PHP and other language like JavaScript.

A new method `call()` binds the anonymous function to some object and calls it with any given parameter.

```
public mixed Closure::call ( object $newthis [, mixed $... ] )
```

An example usage would be a class `Sample` which returns a sample string, which then will be reused in the closure itself.

```
class Sample {
    protected $value;

    public function __construct($value) {
        $this->value = $value;
    }

    public function getValue() {
        return $this->value;
    }
}

$first = new Sample('first');
$second = new Value('second');

$closure = function ($extraVar1, $extraVar2) { echo $this->getValue().' -
'.$extraVar1.' and '.$extraVar2; };
$closure->call($first, 1, 2);
$closure->call($second, 3, 4);

//results in:
first - 1 and 2
second - 3 and 4
```

Notice that we can pass as many arguments to the call method as we want, as long as we pass the first parameter; we don't need to pass anything else. A crucial thing in this example is using `getValue()` which uses `$this` as a context; this confirms that the closure works as expected later in the results. This behavior is extremely useful when we don't have edit access to the library codebase but we still would want to inject our logic there.

3.1.7. Safer unserialize()

The function `unserialize()` finally has a second argument `$params` introduced, which currently supports `allowed_classes` index only. This key can be either a simple array of allowed classes or a boolean value. This enhancement to unserialization allows us to decode data coming from unknown sources more safely.

```
// this will unserialize everything as before
$data = unserialize($foo);
//same as above:
$data = unserialize($foo, ['allowed_classes' => false]);

// this will convert all objects into __PHP_Incomplete_Class object
$data = unserialize($foo, ['allowed_classes' => false]);
// this will convert all objects except ones of Class1 and Class2 into
__PHP_Incomplete_Class object
$data = unserialize($foo, ['allowed_classes' => ['Class1', 'Class2']]);
```

The disallowed classes will not be converted into proper classes, so their calls of: `_toString()`, `_call()`, `_construct()` or `_destruct()` will also not be called at any time. Which previously could potentially cause some malicious code to run when we weren't aware of the class contents.

3.1.8. Null coalescing (??) operator

The double question mark operator has finally joined the PHP world. This is a shorthand of using a ternary in conjunction with `isset()`. We can use nested coalescing operators within the same line to check the first option, then the second and after pick the default if both of the first values are null or not set.

```
$user = $_GET['user'] ?? $_SESSION['user'] ?? 'guest';
//the above is equivalent to:
$user = isset($_GET['user']) ?
   $_GET['user'] :
   (isset($_SESSION['user']) ? $_SESSION['user'] : 'guest');
```

Bear in mind that in the above example we will only return a string of 'guest' if both of the SESSION and GET param are not set. If we want to include the check for 0 or empty strings then we should use ?: so called: Ternary Operator. Another difference between ?? and ?: is that Null Coalescing operator will not output an E_NOTICE when you have an undefined variable.

```
$first = ''; // or 0

$second = $first ?? 'first';
// $second is '' or 0

$third = $first ?: 'first';
// $third is 'first'
```

3.1.9. Spaceship (<=>) operator

The second new operator is a tactical force for comparing two expressions, mainly used in custom sorting mechanisms. Hence it returns 0 (if both sides are equal), -1 (if the left expression is smaller) and 1 (if the expression on the right is smaller).

```
//numbers
echo 3 <=> 3; // 0
echo 2 <=> 3; // -1
echo 3 <=> 2; // 1

// Strings
echo 'a' <=> 'a'; // 0
echo 'a' <=> 'b'; // -1
echo 'b' <=> 'a'; // 1
```

Spaceship operator is a shortcut for doing a repetitive check for special sorting methods like these shown below:

```
function sortIndicator($a, $b) {
    if ($a > $b) {
        return -1;
    } else {
        return 1;
    }
    return 0;
}
```

3.1.10. Unicode codepoint escape syntax

PHP7 now lets you use the unicode characters escaped by UTF-8 in the hexadecimal format. What does it mean? In simple words: we get the opportunity to use more UTF special characters than before. So before we had chance to use entities to display weird characters like `&pound;` to display £, whereas now we can use the standard way of using the unicode in hex format, for instance: `\u{00A3}` will also display a pound sign.

```
echo 'here is a currency sign: &pound;'
//will result: here is a currency sign: £

echo "here is also a currency sign: \u{00A3}"
//will result: here is also a currency sign: £
```

As you have noticed you can select any other special character by changing `00A3` with any other value. A list of sample available hex unicode characters is available under: *https://www.w3schools.com/↪ charsets/ref_utf_arrows.asp*. Just make sure you are using strings in double quotes, otherwise it won't be picked up correctly.

3.1.11. error_clear_last()

A new function `error_clear_last()` was added to the Error Handling Functions. This particular mechanism clears out the most recent error by making it unavailable to retrieve again by `error_get_last()`.

```
function error_handler($code, $message, $file, $line) {
    echo: 'new error has occurred:'.PHP_EOL;
    var_dump(error_get_last());

    error_clear_last();
    echo 'error cleared'.PHP_EOL;
    var_dump(error_get_last());
}

set_error_handler('error_handler');

@$a = $b;

//will result in:
new error has occurred:
```

```
array(4) {
  ["type"]=>
  int(8)
  ["message"]=>
  string(21) "Undefined variable: b"
  ["file"]=>
  string(9) "%s"
  ["line"]=>
  int(6)
}
error cleared
NULL
```

3.1.12. DateTime and date() with milliseconds

A small update has been made to both `DateTime` object and `date()` function, which will allow us to display milliseconds (three additional numbers after the decimal point of the seconds). We can use a new constant `DateTime::RFC3339_EXTENDED` with conjunction of `DateTime format()` method for full date time or `DATE::RFC3339_EXTENDED`. We can also use a new `date()` alpha character: "v" to manually insert just the milliseconds in the place we want to.

```
//DateTime
$date = new DateTime();
echo $date->format(DateTime::RFC3339_EXTENDED);
//outputs:
2018-10-15T15:52:01.000+00:00

//date
echo date('Y-m-d H:i:s.v');
//outputs
2018-10-15 15:52:02.000
```

3.1.13. Huge Pages and File Base Opcache

Opcode cache gets a little performance boost from the added Huge Pages support. In a nutshell, Huge Pages is a mechanism of allocating memory by allowing larger chunks of packets to be claimed in bigger blocks than initial.

```
//php.ini file:
;Enables or disables copying of PHP code into HUGE PAGES.
; Requires appropriate OS configuration but will improve performance.
opcache.huge_code_pages=1
```

You will also need to compile PHP with proper configuration option included:

```
./configure --enable-huge-code-pages
```

The file-based cache has also been introduced and can be used as either primary or a secondary level of cache. This obviously will improve the overall efficiency of our code execution.

```
//php.ini file
; Enables and sets the second level cache directory.
; It should improve performance when SHM memory is full, at server restart or
; SHM reset. The default "" disables file based caching.
opcache.file_cache=1

; Enables or disables opcode caching in shared memory.
opcache.file_cache_only=0

; Enables or disables checksum validation when script loaded from file cache.
opcache.file_cache_consistency_checks=1
```

3.1.14. SSL alpn_protocols

The new added "alpn_protocols" in SSL context option allows encrypted client/server streams to negotiate alternative protocols using the ALPN TLS extension when built against OpenSSL 1.0.2 or newer. This context confronts to the HTTP/2 support in Apache servers. Negotiated protocol is available through `stream_get_meta_data()` function output.

3.1.15. Rusage support for pcntl package

The pcntl_* functions relate to parallel PHP processes via simple, easy to implement and run PCNTL protocol with high effect. The above extension imitates Unix style of process creation, execution, signal handling and process termination. The functions: `pcntl_wait()` and `pcntl_waitpid()`, deal with waiting or returning the status of forked child globally or by the specified pid argument so: process ID. Rusage is a resource usage, which we can provide to make the call even more specific than before. The current resource usages can be obtained by `getrusage()` function.

3.1.16. ReflectionGenerator

The new reflection helper class has been introduced to the language to help out obtain information about the generator itself. But before we even start up listing available methods and examples, we need to explain a bit the component tied very closely to the reflection generator itself (if you know what is: `yield`, then you can easily skip the next subchapter).

3.1.17. yield

Alright, so this isn't really a PHP 7 feature, however 9 out of 10 developers will have no idea when somebody says: "hey why haven't you used a yield here?" "wait what?". Yields have been added in PHP 5 and are mainly used with reflection mechanisms. Yield behaves very similarly to the return keyword, but with one small difference. Yield doesn't stop the execution of the function, instead it pauses it and return as an array in buffer as output if we will have a yield used more than once. Here is a small example:

```php
function sampleIteration() {
    for ($i = 0; $i < 3; $i++) {
        yield $i;
    }
}

//link function to the variable which then will loop through
$generator = sampleIteration();
foreach ($generator as $value) {
    echo "$value\n";
}
//will output:
```

```
0
1
2
```

Because we have used yield instead return we have received an array of values instead of just the number: 0. Notice that yield created an array when used more than once; if we had just one yield key, then we would just get that one value instead of the array. In a nutshell yield returns a value but it won't stop the function context from execution and will offer us a list of variables as function output at the end.

3.1.18. ReflectionGenerator continued

Welcome back! Once we are more familiar with yields and what they are for, we can take a closer look at a new reflection class which will gather the reporting information about the generator. The available methods are:

- getExecutingFile() - returns a file name of a currently executing generator;

- getExecutingLine() - returns a line number of a currently executing generator;

- getExecutingGenerator() - gets the Generator object;

- getFunction() - outputs the function name;

- getThis() - obtains a value of $this from the class;

- getTrace() - gets a stack trace of the run generator.

Most of the methods are simple to use: gathering function name, file or line, one of the most useful ones are getThis() if we want just plain $this variable out of the class or getTrace(). We will demonstrate how to use the last method.

```
function first() {
    yield 1;
}
```

```php
function second()
{
    yield from first();
}

function third()
{
    yield from second();
}

$generator = third();
$generator->valid(); // start the generator

var_dump((new ReflectionGenerator($generator))->getTrace());

//will output:
array(2) {
  [0]=>
  array(4) {
    ["file"]=>
    string(18) "example.php"
    ["line"]=>
    int(8)
    ["function"]=>
    string(3) "first"
    ["args"]=>
    array(0) {
    }
  }
  [1]=>
  array(4) {
    ["file"]=>
    string(18) "example.php"
    ["line"]=>
    int(12)
    ["function"]=>
    string(3) "second"
    ["args"]=>
    array(0) {
    }
  }
}
```

Notice that we used a combination of yield form to indicate we await the

yield value from the another function. We also started with ->valid()
method which is available when using yields to inform the generator that
we want to intercept the required information.

3.1.19. intdiv()

A new function intdiv() is a special integer division. What does it
make it so special? The integer keyword. Notice that values like 0, 1 or
2.3333 are usually called number not integers. Integers have no values
after comma or dot, but they can still be a positive numbers or a negative
numbers. So in a nutshell intdiv() always displays a result in whole
numbers (integers). intdiv() is also clever enough to cope with
negative dividers and returning arithmetic exceptions when dividing by
zero. Here are some instances of usages:

```
echo intdiv(-10,3); // returns -3
echo intdiv(8, 3); //returns 2
echo intdiv(3, 3); //returns 1
echo intdiv(2, 3); //returns 0
echo intdiv(PHP_INT_MIN, -1); //returns Fatal error: Uncaught ArithmeticError:
Division of PHP_INT_MIN by -1 is not an integer in %s on line 8
echo intdiv(2, 0); //returns Fatal error: Uncaught DivisionByZeroError: Division by
zero in %s on line 9
```

3.1.20. preg_replace_callback_array()

The new function's behaviour is almost identical to its precursor's:
pref_replace_callback(), but PHP finally gives us an opportunity to
pass multiple patterns linked with specific callbacks.

```
mixed preg_replace_callback_array ( array $patterns_and_callbacks , mixed $subject
[, int $limit = -1 [, int &$count ]] )
```

We can also pass a $limit parameter to set maximum possible
replacements for each patterns in each string (no limit by default), and
$count which will be filled with the number of replacements done.

Before PHP 5.6, we had to write:

```
$htmlString = preg_replace_callback(
```

```
    '/(href="?)(\S+)("?)/i',
    function (&$matches) {
        return $matches[1] . urldecode($matches[2]) . $matches[3];
    },
    $htmlString
);

$htmlString = preg_replace_callback(
    '/(href="?\S+)(%24)(\S+)?"?/i', // %24 = $
    function (&$matches) {
        return urldecode($matches[1] . '$' . $matches[3]);
    },
    $htmlString
);
```

And now we can simply do:

```
$htmlString = preg_replace_callback_array(
    [
        '/(href="?)(\S+)("?)/i' => function (&$matches) {
            return $matches[1] . urldecode($matches[2]) . $matches[3];
        },
        '/(href="?\S+)(%24)(\S+)?"?/i' => function (&$matches) {
            return urldecode($matches[1] . '$' . $matches[3]);
        }
    ],
    $htmlString
);
```

3.1.21. getrusage()

Another new function added in PHP 7 is `getrusage()`, which returns a list of current resource usages in form of the associative array container data returned from the system.

```
array getrusage ([ int $who = 0 ] )
```

If `$who` parameter is passed as 2, it will return the data from the system call; if the value is 1, then it will be called with RUSAGE_CHILDREN. The output will vary between the systems, but on a Windows server `getrusage()` will only return:

- "ru_stime.tv_sec"

- "ru_stime.tv_usec"

- "ru_utime.tv_sec"

- "ru_utime.tv_usec"

- "ru_majflt" (if $who is RUSAGE_SELF)

- "ru_maxrss" (if $who is RUSAGE_SELF)

Sample regular output might be:

```
$dat = getrusage();
echo $dat["ru_oublock"];      // number of block output operations
echo $dat["ru_inblock"];      // number of block input operations
echo $dat["ru_msgsnd"];        // number of IPC messages sent
echo $dat["ru_msgrcv"];        // number of IPC messages received
echo $dat["ru_maxrss"];        // maximum resident set size
echo $dat["ru_ixrss"];        // integral shared memory size
echo $dat["ru_idrss"];        // integral unshared data size
echo $dat["ru_minflt"];        // number of page reclaims (soft page faults)
echo $dat["ru_majflt"];        // number of page faults (hard page faults)
echo $dat["ru_nsignals"];      // number of signals received
echo $dat["ru_nvcsw"];        // number of voluntary context switches
echo $dat["ru_nivcsw"];        // number of involuntary context switches
echo $dat["ru_nswap"];        // number of swaps
echo $dat["ru_utime.tv_usec"]; // user time used (microseconds)
echo $dat["ru_utime.tv_sec"];  // user time used (seconds)
echo $dat["ru_stime.tv_usec"]; // system time used (microseconds)
```

Please, be aware that this function returns rusage of the current process. In a web environment where you have long running apache processes that serve several requests with PHP executions, this will return cumulative timings and is therefore not suitable for telling how much user time your used. The best you can do is call getrusage() once at the beginning and once at the end and then calculate the difference.

3.1.22. ZLib inflate_* and deflate_*

There are 4 new functions in total added to the ZLib package: `inflate_init()` for creating incremental inflate object, `inflate_add()` for adding contents to the new returned context and `defalte_init()` together with `deflate_add()` required for encoding the data via the same incremental way. All of these `_init()` functions take just one argument which is a ZLIB encoding constant and all of the `_add()` functions take 3 arguments: context, data and ZLIB flush mode constant. Please, be aware that the header information from GZIP compressed data is not available.

```
// GZIP compression:
$deflateContext = deflate_init(ZLIB_ENCODING_GZIP);
$compressed = deflate_add($deflateContext, "Here we start", ZLIB_NO_FLUSH);
$compressed .= deflate_add($deflateContext, ", then we continue",
ZLIB_NO_FLUSH);
$compressed .= deflate_add($deflateContext, ", and we finish.", ZLIB_FINISH);?>

// GZIP decompression:
$inflateContext = inflate_init(ZLIB_ENCODING_GZIP);
$uncompressed = inflate_add($inflateContext, $compressed, ZLIB_NO_FLUSH);
$uncompressed .= inflate_add($inflateContext, NULL, ZLIB_FINISH);
echo $uncompressed;

//will output
Here we start, then we continue, and we finish.
```

3.1.23. ZipArchive setCompressionName() and setComporessionIndex()

The two freshly implemented mechanisms set the type of the compression of a single entry defined by either name or by its index.

```
bool ZipArchive::setCompressionName ( string $name , int $comp_method [, int
$comp_flags = 0 ] )

bool ZipArchive::setCompressionName ( string $name , int $comp_method [, int
$comp_flags = 0 ] )
```

Both of these methods can be used at the same time; the only vital thing is to keep the same key name, for instance we can have 4 strings in simple zip file like so:

```
$zip = new ZipArchive();
$res = $zip->open('test.zip', ZipArchive::CREATE);
if ($res === TRUE) {
    $zip->addFromString('first', 'First text');
    $zip->addFromString('second', 'Some other text');
    $zip->addFromString('third', 'index based text');
    $zip->addFromString('fourth', 'another index text');

    $zip->setCompressionName('first', ZipArchive::CM_STORE);
    $zip->setCompressionName('second', ZipArchive::CM_DEFLATE);
    $zip->setCompressionIndex(2, ZipArchive::CM_STORE); //this will apply to the
key 'third'
    $zip->setCompressionIndex(3, ZipArchive::CM_DEFLATE); //this will apply to the
key 'fourth'
    $zip->close();
    echo 'file generated correctly';
} else {
    echo 'something went wrong';
}
```

3.1.24. Catchable Errors

We are finally able to catch build-in PHP Errors and throw our own Error objects in PHP 7. A standard PHP Error class implements new `Throwable` interference and other error types extend the base of the Error instance. The other errors are:

- TypeError

- ParseError

- AssertionError

- ArithmeticError

- DivisionByZeroError

A sample usage of all of the possible Error is presented below:

```php
$classObject = new class() {
    public function done() {
        echo 'works';
    }
};

try {
    $classObject->done(); // works
    $classObject->done2();
} catch (Error $e) {
    echo 'done2 has caused an error';
}

//will output
done2 has caused an error
```

3.1.25. Dynamic static calls

If we would ever want to access any static variable or method from the class object using the string name of the class, now we can! Just call `'MyClass'::$property` like below:

```php
class MyClass {
    public static $property = 'some value';
}
echo 'MyClass'::$property;

//will output
some value
```

3.2. Fixed bugs

PHP 7.0 has really focused on fixing crucial aspects of the language, so some of these bugs might as well be counted towards as feature updates. Overall PHP 7.0 has targeted over 921 bugs in total.

#75880. When you are using casting to array syntax, so: `(array)$object`, then any of integer keys will be casted to proper integers, even when they were initially a string numbers.

```
$obj = '{"300": {"id": "foo"}}';
$obj = json_decode($obj);
$obj = (array)$obj;
var_dump($obj); // array (size=1) '300' => string 'foo' (length=3)
var_dump($obj[300]); // 'foo'
```

#74862. Private `__clone` magic methods are no longer displaying a Fatal Error when we perform a clone from the same class within its context.

```
class MyClass {
    private function __clone() { }

    private function __construct() { }

    public function cloneIt()
    {
        $a = clone $this;

        return $a;
    }
}

//this will no longer break in PHP7
new MyClass()->cloneIt()
```

#73163. Fixed infinite loop, when you have used an undefined constant as default function argument parameter.

```
function doSomething(string $value = UNDEFINED_CONST) {
}

set_error_handler(function() {
    throw new Exception();
});

doSomething();
```

#72159. Importing class with the same name within the namespace will now display a new error: *"Fatal error: Cannot declare class* `Package\Bar` *because the name is already in use"* previously it was just overriding the class contents with a new one.

#71914 Function arguments passed by reference are losing sync when using a switch loop.

```
function bug(&$value) {
    switch ($value) {
    case "abc":
        $value = true;
        break;
    }
}

echo bug('abc');
//will now return:
true
```

#72119. Classes that implement methods from interfaces no longer have to have the same default argument values as in interface.

```
interface MyInterface {
    public function bar(array $baz = null);
}

class MyClass implements MyInterface {
    public function bar(array $baz = [])
    {

    }
}

//before the PHP 7 it would cause interface mismatch error:
Fatal error: Declaration of MyClass ::bar(array $baz = Array) must be compatible
with MyInterface ::bar(array $baz = NULL) in /in/Vhad on line 7

//this now work just fine and will not produce any error
```

#71737. Fixed memory leakage when a closure is used within the class and when $this is used as an argument to that anonymous function.

#70997. Overwritten class child constant does not override the reference within the parent class, if parent class is using that constant. For instance:

```
class Parent {
    const TEST = 'parent';

    public function test()
    {
        var_dump(static::TEST);
    }
}

class Child extends Parent {
    const TEST = 'child';

    public function test()
    {
        A::test();
    }
}

$a = new Child();
$a->test();
//will produce now 'child' instead 'parent'
```

#70967. Exceptions and Fatal Errors are now being thrown properly within __toString(), which used to prohibit to display any error.

```
echo new MyClass {
    function __toString() {
        return some_invalid(1); // invalid function name
    }
};
```

```
//previously it was returning:
Fatal error: Method MyClass@anonymous::__toString() must not throw an exception

//now it will produce:
Method MyClass::__toString() must not throw an exception. Fatal error: Call to
undefined function some_invalid() in file.php on line 24
```

#70223. Strict comparison between empty strings and integer keys in arrays do not crash anymore PHP with segmentation fault as they were on 5.x versions.

```
var_dump([0 => 0] === ["" => 0]);
```

More of the covered bugs can be found in the Change Log subsection.

3.3. Deprecated elements

3.3.1. Old constructors

Old school constructors (pre PHP 5) so the methods that have the same name as the class name), are now marked as deprecated and will be removed in the near future.

```
class MyClass {
    function MyClass () {
      //constructor code which is marked as deprecated
    }
}
```

3.3.2. password_hash() salt

The argument of `$salt` was deprecated mainly due to salt was generating insecure passwords. The function without the salt is already providing a secure cryptography, hence the custom salt should no longer be needed.

3.3.3. Static calls

PHP is going to be very strict in terms of OO principles; this is why any static calls to the nonstatic methods will be deprecated and will be removed completely before PHP 8 version.

```
class MyClass {
    public function myMethod() {
        echo 'My sample output';
    }
}


MyClass::myMethod();

//will output
Deprecated: Non-static method MyClass::myMethod() should not be called statically
in - on line 8
My sample output
```

3.3.4. ldap_sort()

The LDAP sorting function is also going to be dropped in near future. The main reason is the deprecated C sorting function, which is used for ldap_sort(), and the fact that nobody from the PHP crew knows exactly how that internal C mechanism works. Another issue are many troubles with sorting outcome which aren't something a regular user expects from it. The alternative for now will be to retrieve all records and sort it via PHP built-in sorting mechanisms. The PHP team is also working on alternative method in PHP 8; however in the meantime you can use a solution from Zend Framework codebase and package: *Zend\Ldap\Collection\DefaultIterator* which contains method: `sort()`. *https://github.com/zendframework/zend-ldap/blob/master/src/↪ Collection/DefaultIterator.php#L379-L403* .

3.4. Removed elements and SAPIs

- ereg

- mssql

- mysql

- sybase_ct

- aolserver

- apache

- apache_hooks

- apache2filter

- caudium

- continuity

- isapi

- milter

- nsapi

- phttpd

- pi3web

- roxen

- thttpd

- tux

- webjames

3.5. Change log

17 Dec 2015, PHP 7.0.1

- Core:
  . Fixed bug #71105 (Format String Vulnerability in Class Name Error Message).
    (andrew at jmpesp dot org)
  . Fixed bug #70831 (Compile fails on system with 160 CPUs).
    (Daniel Axtens)
  . Fixed bug #71006 (symbol referencing errors on Sparc/Solaris). (Dmitry)
  . Fixed bug #70997 (When using parentClass::

instead of parent::, static context changed). (Dmitry)
  . Fixed bug #70970 (Segfault when combining error handler with output buffering). (Laruence)
  . Fixed bug #70967 (Weird error handling for __toString when Error is thrown). (Laruence)
  . Fixed bug #70958 (Invalid opcode while using ::class as trait method paramater default value). (Laruence)
  . Fixed bug #70944 (try{ } finally{} can create

infinite chains of
   exceptions). (Laruence)
 . Fixed bug #70931 (Two errors messages are in conflict). (dams, Laruence)
 . Fixed bug #70904 (yield from incorrectly marks valid generator as finished).
   (Bob)
 . Fixed bug #70899 (buildconf failure in extensions). (Bob, Reeze)
 . Fixed bug #61751 (SAPI build problem on AIX: Undefined symbol:
   php_register_internal_extensions). (Lior Kaplan)
 . Fixed \int (or generally every scalar type name with leading backslash)
   to not be accepted as type name. (Bob)
 . Fixed exception not being thrown immediately into a generator yielding
   from an array. (Bob)
 . Fixed bug #70987 (static::class within Closure::call() causes segfault).
   (Andrea)
 . Fixed bug #71013 (Incorrect exception handler with yield from). (Bob)
 . Fixed double free in error condition of format printer. (Bob)

- CLI server:
 . Fixed bug #71005 (Segfault in php_cli_server_dispatch_router()). (Adam)

- Intl:
 . Fixed bug #71020 (Use after free in Collator::sortWithSortKeys).
   (emmanuel dot law at gmail dot com, Laruence)

- Mysqlnd:
 . Fixed bug #68077 (LOAD DATA LOCAL INFILE / open_basedir restriction).
   (Laruence)
 . Fixed bug #68344 (MySQLi does not provide way to disable peer certificate
   validation) by introducing MYSQLI_CLIENT_SSL_DONT_VERIFY_SERVER_CERT
   connection flag. (Andrey)

- OCI8:
 . Fixed LOB implementation size_t/zend_long mismatch reported
   by gcov. (Senthil)

- Opcache:
 . Fixed #71024 (Unable to use PHP 7.0 x64 side-by-side with PHP 5.6 x32 on
   the same server). (Anatol)
 . Fixed bug #70991 (zend_file_cache.c:710: error: array type has incomplete
   element type). (Laruence)
 . Fixed bug #70977 (Segmentation fault with opcache.huge_code_pages=1).
   (Laruence)

- Phpdbg:
 . Fixed stderr being written to stdout. (Bob)

- Reflection:
 . Fixed bug #71018 (ReflectionProperty::setValue() behavior changed).
   (Laruence)
 . Fixed bug #70982 (setStaticPropertyValue behaviors inconsistently with

5.6). (Laruence)

- SPL:
 . Fixed bug #71028 (Undefined index with ArrayIterator). (Laruence)

- SQLite3:
 . Fixed bug #71049 (SQLite3Stmt::execute() releases bound parameter instead
   of internal buffer). (Laruence)

- Standard:
 . Fixed bug #70999 (php_random_bytes: called object is not a function).
   (Scott)
 . Fixed bug #70960 (ReflectionFunction for array_unique returns wrong number
   of parameters). (Laruence)

- Streams/Socket:
 . Add IPV6_V6ONLY constant / make it usable in stream contexts. (Bob)

- Soap:
 . Fixed bug #70993 (Array key references break argument processing).
   (Laruence)

- PDO_Firebird:
 . Fixed bug #60052 (Integer returned as a 64bit integer on X64_86). (Mariuz)

03 Dec 2015, PHP 7.0.0

- Core:
 . Fixed bug #70947 (INI parser segfault with INI_SCANNER_TYPED). (Laruence)
 . Fixed bug #70914 (zend_throw_or_error() format string vulnerability).
   (Taoguang Chen)
 . Fixed bug #70912 (Null ptr dereference instantiating class with invalid
   array property). (Laruence)
 . Fixed bug #70895, #70898 (null ptr deref and segfault with crafted calable).
   (Anatol, Laruence)
 . Fixed bug #70249 (Segmentation fault while running PHPUnit tests on
   phpBB 3.2-dev). (Laruence)
 . Fixed bug #70805 (Segmentation faults whilst running Drupal 8 test suite).
   (Dmitry, Laruence)
 . Fixed bug #70842 (Persistent Stream Segmentation Fault). (Caleb Champlin)
 . Fixed bug #70862 (Several functions do not check return code of
   php_stream_copy_to_mem()). (Anatol)
 . Fixed bug #70863 (Incorect logic to increment_function for proxy objects).
   (Anatol)
 . Fixed bug #70323 (Regression in zend_fetch_debug_backtrace() can cause
   segfaults). (Aharvey, Laruence)
 . Fixed bug #70873 (Regression on private static properties access).
   (Laruence)
 . Fixed bug #70748 (Segfault in ini_lex () at Zend/zend_ini_scanner.l).
   (Laruence)
 . Fixed bug #70689 (Exception handler does not work as expected). (Laruence)
 . Fixed bug #70430 (Stack buffer overflow in zend_language_parser()). (Nikita)

. Fixed bug #70782 (null ptr deref and segfault (zend_get_class_fetch_type)).
(Nikita)
. Fixed bug #70785 (Infinite loop due to exception during identical
comparison). (Laruence)
. Fixed bug #70630 (Closure::call/bind() crash with ReflectionFunction->
getClosure()). (Dmitry, Bob)
. Fixed bug #70662 (Duplicate array key via undefined index error handler).
(Nikita)
. Fixed bug #70681 (Segfault when binding $this of internal instance method
to null). (Nikita)
. Fixed bug #70685 (Segfault for getClosure() internal method rebind with
invalid $this). (Nikita)
. Added zend_internal_function.reserved[] fields. (Dmitry)
. Fixed bug #70557 (Memleak on return type verifying failed). (Laruence)
. Fixed bug #70555 (fun_get_arg() on unsetted vars return UNKNOW). (Laruence)
. Fixed bug #70548 (Redundant information printed in case of uncaught engine
exception). (Laruence)
. Fixed bug #70547 (unsetting function variables corrupts backtrace).
(Laruence)
. Fixed bug #70528 (assert() with instanceof adds apostrophes around class
name). (Laruence)
. Fixed bug #70481 (Memory leak in auto_global_copy_ctor() in ZTS build).
(Laruence)
. Fixed bug #70431 (Memory leak in php_ini.c).
(Senthil, Laruence)
. Fixed bug #70478 (**= does no longer work). (Bob)
. Fixed bug #70398 (SIGSEGV, Segmentation fault zend_ast_destroy_ex).
(Dmitry, Bob, Laruence)
. Fixed bug #70332 (Wrong behavior while returning reference on object).
(Laruence, Dmitry)
. Fixed bug #70300 (Syntactical inconsistency with new group use syntax).
(marcio dot web2 at gmail dot com)
. Fixed bug #70321 (Magic getter breaks reference to array property).
(Laruence)
. Fixed bug #70187 (Notice: unserialize(): Unexpected end of serialized
data). (Dmitry)
. Fixed bug #70145 (From field incorrectly parsed from headers). (Anatol)
. Fixed bug #70370 (Bundled libtool.m4 doesn't handle FreeBSD 10 when
building extensions). (Adam)
. Fixed bug causing exception traces with anon classes to be truncated. (Bob)
. Fixed bug #70397 (Segmentation fault when using Closure::call and yield).
(Bob)
. Fixed bug #70299 (Memleak while assigning object offsetGet result).
(Laruence)
. Fixed bug #70288 (Apache crash related to ZEND_SEND_REF). (Laruence)
. Fixed bug #70262 (Accessing array crashes PHP 7.0beta3).
(Laruence, Dmitry)

. Fixed bug #70258 (Segfault if do_resize fails to allocated memory).
(Laruence)
. Fixed bug #70253 (segfault at _efree () in zend_alloc.c:1389). (Laruence)
. Fixed bug #70240 (Segfault when doing unset($var());). (Laruence)
. Fixed bug #70223 (Incrementing value returned by magic getter). (Laruence)
. Fixed bug #70215 (Segfault when __invoke is static). (Bob)
. Fixed bug #70207 (Finally is broken with opcache). (Laruence, Dmitry)
. Fixed bug #70173 (ZVAL_COPY_VALUE_EX broken for 32bit Solaris Sparc).
(Laruence, cmb)
. Fixed bug #69487 (SAPI may truncate POST data). (cmb)
. Fixed bug #70198 (Checking liveness does not work as expected).
(Shafreeck Sea, Anatol Belski)
. Fixed bug #70241,#70293 (Skipped assertions affect Generator returns). (Bob)
. Fixed bug #70239 (Creating a huge array doesn't result in exhausted,
but segfault). (Laruence, Anatol)
. Fixed "finally" issues. (Nikita, Dmitry)
. Fixed bug #70098 (Real memory usage doesn't decrease). (Dmitry)
. Fixed bug #70159 (__CLASS__ is lost in closures). (Julien)
. Fixed bug #70156 (Segfault in zend_find_alias_name). (Laruence)
. Fixed bug #70124 (null ptr deref / seg fault in ZEND_HANDLE_EXCEPTION).
(Laruence)
. Fixed bug #70117 (Unexpected return type error). (Laruence)
. Fixed bug #70106 (Inheritance by anonymous class). (Bob)
. Fixed bug #69674 (SIGSEGV array.c:953). (cmb)
. Fixed bug #70164 (__COMPILER_HALT_OFFSET__ under namespace is not defined).
(Bob)
. Fixed bug #70108 (sometimes empty $_SERVER['QUERY_STRING']). (Anatol)
. Fixed bug #70179 ($this refcount issue). (Bob)
. Fixed bug #69896 ('asm' operand has impossible constraints). (Anatol)
. Fixed bug #70183 (null pointer deref (segfault) in zend_eval_const_expr).
(Hugh Davenport)
. Fixed bug #70182 (Segfault in ZEND_ASSIGN_DIV_SPEC_CV_UNUSED_HANDLER).
(Hugh Davenport)
. Fixed bug #69793 (Remotely triggerable stack exhaustion via recursive
method calls). (Stas)
. Fixed bug #69892 (Different arrays compare indentical due to integer key
truncation). (Nikita)
. Fixed bug #70121 (unserialize() could lead to unexpected methods execution
/ NULL pointer deref). (Stas)
. Fixed bug #70089 (segfault at ZEND_FETCH_DIM_W_SPEC_VAR_CONST_HANDLER ()).
(Laruence)
. Fixed bug #70057 (Build failure on 32-bit Mac OS X 10.6.8: recursive

inlining). (Laruence)
. Fixed bug #70012 (Exception lost with nested finally block). (Laruence)
. Fixed bug #69996 (Changing the property of a cloned object affects the
    original). (Dmitry, Laruence)
. Fixed bug #70083 (Use after free with assign by ref to overloaded objects).
    (Bob)
. Fixed bug #70006 (cli - function with default arg = STDOUT crash output).
    (Laruence)
. Fixed bug #69521 (Segfault in gc_collect_cycles()).
    (arjen at react dot com, Laruence)
. Improved zend_string API. (Francois Laupretre)
. Fixed bug #69955 (Segfault when trying to combine [] and assign-op on
ArrayAccess object). (Laruence)
. Fixed bug #69957 (Different ways of handling div/mod/intdiv). (Bob)
. Fixed bug #69900 (Too long timeout on pipes). (Anatol)
. Fixed bug #69872 (uninitialised value in strtr with array). (Laruence)
. Fixed bug #69868 (Invalid read of size 1 in zend_compile_short_circuiting).
    (Laruence)
. Fixed bug #69849 (Broken output of apache_request_headers). (Kalle)
. Fixed bug #69840 (iconv_substr() doesn't work with UTF-16BE). (Kalle)
. Fixed bug #69823 (PHP 7.0.0alpha1 segmentation fault when exactly 33
    extensions are loaded). (Laruence)
. Fixed bug #69805 (null ptr deref and seg fault in zend_resolve_class_name).
    (Laruence)
. Fixed bug #69802 (Reflection on Closure::__invoke borks type hint class
    name). (Dmitry)
. Fixed bug #69761 (Serialization of anonymous classes should be prevented).
    (Laruence)
. Fixed bug #69551 (parse_ini_file() and parse_ini_string() segmentation
    fault). (Christoph M. Becker)
. Fixed bug #69781 (phpinfo() reports Professional Editions of Windows
    7/8/8.1/10 as "Business"). (Christian Wenz)
. Fixed bug #69835 (phpinfo() does not report many Windows SKUs).
    (Christian Wenz)
. Fixed bug #69889 (Null coalesce operator doesn't work for string offsets).
    (Nikita)
. Fixed bug #69891 (Unexpected array comparison result). (Nikita)
. Fixed bug #69892 (Different arrays compare indentical due to integer key
    truncation). (Nikita)
. Fixed bug #69893 (Strict comparison between integer and empty string keys
    crashes). (Nikita)
. Fixed bug #69767 (Default parameter value with wrong type segfaults).
    (cmb, Laruence)
. Fixed bug #69756 (Fatal error: Nesting level too deep - recursive dependency
    ? with ===). (Dmitry, Laruence)
. Fixed bug #69758 (Item added to array not being removed by array_pop/shift
). (Laruence)

. Fixed bug #68475 (Add support for $callable() sytnax with 'Class::method').
    (Julien, Aaron Piotrowski)
. Fixed bug #69485 (Double free on zend_list_dtor). (Laruence)
. Fixed bug #69427 (Segfault on magic method __call of private method in
    superclass). (Laruence)
. Improved __call() and __callStatic() magic method handling. Now they are
    called in a stackless way using ZEND_CALL_TRAMPOLINE opcode, without
    additional stack frame. (Laruence, Dmitry)
. Optimized strings concatenation. (Dmitry, Laruence)
. Fixed weird operators behavior. Division by zero now emits warning and
    returns +/-INF, modulo by zero and intdid() throws an exception, shifts
    by negative offset throw exceptions. Compile-time evaluation of division
    by zero is disabled. (Dmitry, Andrea, Nikita)
. Fixed bug #69371 (Hash table collision leads to inaccessible array keys).
    (Laruence)
. Fixed bug #68933 (Invalid read of size 8 in zend_std_read_property).
    (Laruence, arjen at react dot com)
. Fixed bug #68252 (segfault in Zend/zend_hash.c in function
    _zend_hash_del_el). (Laruence)
. Fixed bug #65598 (Closure executed via static autoload incorrectly marked as
    static). (Nikita)
. Fixed bug #66811 (Cannot access static::class in lambda, writen outside of a
    class). (Nikita)
. Fixed bug #69568 (call a private function in closure failed). (Nikita)
. Added PHP_INT_MIN constant. (Andrea)
. Added Closure::call() method. (Andrea)
. Fixed bug #67959 (Segfault when calling phpversion('spl')). (Florian)
. Implemented the RFC `Catchable "Call to a member function bar() on a
    non-object"`. (Timm)
. Added options parameter for unserialize allowing to specify acceptable
    classes
(https://wiki.php.net/rfc/secure_unserialize).
(Stas)
. Fixed bug #63734 (Garbage collector can free zvals that are still
    referenced). (Dmitry)
. Removed ZEND_ACC_FINAL_CLASS, promoting ZEND_ACC_FINAL as final class
    modifier. (Guilherme Blanco)
. is_long() & is_integer() is now an alias of is_int(). (Kalle)
. Implemented FR #55467 (phpinfo: PHP Variables with $ and single quotes). (Kalle)
. Added ?? operator. (Andrea)
. Added <=> operator. (Andrea)
. Added \u{xxxxx} Unicode Codepoint Escape Syntax. (Andrea)
. Fixed oversight where define() did not support arrays yet const syntax did.
    (Andrea, Dmitry)
. Use "integer" and "float" instead of "long" and "double" in ZPP, type hint
    and conversion error messages. (Andrea)
. Implemented FR #55428
(E_RECOVERABLE_ERROR when output buffering

in output
buffering handler). (Kalle)
. Removed scoped calls of non-static methods from an incompatible $this
context. (Nikita)
. Removed support for #-style comments in ini files. (Nikita)
. Removed support for assigning the result of new by reference. (Nikita)
. Invalid octal literals in source code now produce compile errors, fixes
PHPSadness #31. (Andrea)
. Removed dl() function on fpm-fcgi. (Nikita)
. Removed support for hexadecimal numeric strings. (Nikita)
. Removed obsolete extensions and SAPIs. See the full list in UPGRADING. (Anatol)
. Added NULL byte protection to exec, system and passthru. (Yasuo)
. Added error_clear_last() function. (Reeze Xia)
. Fixed bug #68797 (Number 2.2250738585072012e-308 converted incorrectly).
(Anatol)
. Improved zend_qsort(using hybrid sorting algo) for better performance,
and also renamed zend_qsort to zend_sort. (Laruence)
. Added stable sorting algo zend_insert_sort. (Laruence)
. Improved zend_memnchr(using sunday algo) for better performance. (Laruence)
. Implemented the RFC `Scalar Type Declarations v0.5`. (Anthony)
. Implemented the RFC `Group Use Declarations`. (Marcio)
. Implemented the RFC `Continue Output Buffering`. (Mike)
. Implemented the RFC `Constructor behaviour of internal classes`. (Dan, Dmitry)
. Implemented the RFC `Fix "foreach" behavior`. (Dmitry)
. Implemented the RFC `Generator Delegation`. (Bob)
. Implemented the RFC `Anonymous Class Support`. (Joe, Nikita, Dmitry)
. Implemented the RFC `Context Sensitive Lexer`. (Marcio Almada)
. Fixed bug #69511 (Off-by-one buffer overflow in php_sys_readlink).
(Jan Starke, Anatol)

- CLI server:
. Fixed bug #68291 (404 on urls with '+'). (cmb)
. Fixed bug #66606 (Sets HTTP_CONTENT_TYPE but not CONTENT_TYPE).
(wusuopu, cmb)
. Fixed bug #70264 (CLI server directory traversal). (cmb)
. Fixed bug #69655 (php -S changes MKCALENDAR request method to MKCOL). (cmb)
. Fixed bug #64878 (304 responses return Content-Type header). (cmb)
. Refactor MIME type handling to use a hash table instead of linear search.
(Adam)
. Update the MIME type list from the one shipped by Apache HTTPD. (Adam)
. Added support for SEARCH WebDav method. (Mats Lindh)

- COM:
. Fixed bug #69939 (Casting object to bool

returns false). (Kalle)

- Curl:
. Fixed bug #70330 (Segmentation Fault with multiple "curl_copy_handle").
(Laruence)
. Fixed bug #70163 (curl_setopt_array() type confusion). (Laruence)
. Fixed bug #70065 (curl_getinfo() returns corrupted values). (Anatol)
. Fixed bug #69831 (Segmentation fault in curl_getinfo). (im dot denisenko at
yahoo dot com)
. Fixed bug #68937 (Segfault in curl_multi_exec). (Laruence)
. Removed support for unsafe file uploads. (Nikita)

- Date:
. Fixed bug #70245 (strtotime does not emit warning when 2nd parameter is
object or string). (cmb)
. Fixed bug #70266 (DateInterval::__construct.interval_spec is not supposed to
be optional). (cmb)
. Fixed bug #70277 (new DateTimeZone($foo) is ignoring text after null byte).
(cmb)
. Fixed day_of_week function as it could sometimes return negative values
internally. (Derick)
. Removed $is_dst parameter from mktime() and gmmktime(). (Nikita)
. Removed date.timezone warning
(https://wiki.php.net/rfc/date.timezone_warning_removal). (Bob)
. Added "v" DateTime format modifier to get the 3-digit version of fraction
of seconds. (Mariano Iglesias)
. Implemented FR #69089 (Added DateTime::RFC3339_EXTENDED to output in
RFC3339 Extended format which includes fraction of seconds). (Mariano
Iglesias)

- DBA:
. Fixed bug #62490 (dba_delete returns true on missing item (inifile)). (Mike)
. Fixed bug #68711 (useless comparisons). (bugreports at internot dot info)

- DOM:
. Fixed bug #70558 ("Couldn't fetch" error in DOMDocument::registerNodeClass()).
(Laruence)
. Fixed bug #70001 (Assigning to DOMNode::textContent does additional entity
encoding). (cmb)
. Fixed bug #69846 (Segmenation fault (access violation) when iterating over
DOMNodeList). (Anatol Belski)
. Made DOMNode::textContent writeable. (Tjerk)

- EXIF:
. Fixed bug #70385 (Buffer over-read in exif_read_data with TIFF IFD tag byte
value of 32 bytes). (Stas)

- Fileinfo:
. Fixed bug #66242 (libmagic: don't assume char is signed). (ArdB)

- Filter:
  . New FILTER_VALIDATE_DOMAIN and better RFC conformance for FILTER_VALIDATE_URL. (Kevin Dunglas)

- FPM:
  . Fixed bug #70538 ("php-fpm -i" crashes). (rainer dot jung at
      kippdata dot de)
  . Fixed bug #70279 (HTTP Authorization Header is sometimes passed to newer
      reqeusts). (Laruence)
  . Fixed bug #68945 (Unknown admin values segfault pools). (Laruence)
  . Fixed bug #65933 (Cannot specify config lines longer than 1024 bytes). (Chris Wright)
  . Implemented FR #67106 (Split main fpm config). (Elan Ruusamäe, Remi)

- FTP:
  . Fixed bug #69082 (FTPS support on Windows). (Anatol)

- GD:
  . Fixed bug #53156 (imagerectangle problem with point ordering). (cmb)
  . Fixed bug #66387 (Stack overflow with imagefilltoborder). (cmb)
  . Fixed bug #70102 (imagecreatefromwebm() shifts colors). (cmb)
  . Fixed bug #66590 (imagewebp() doesn't pad to even length). (cmb)
  . Fixed bug #66882 (imagerotate by -90 degrees truncates image by 1px). (cmb)
  . Fixed bug #70064 (imagescale(..., IMG_BICUBIC) leaks memory). (cmb)
  . Fixed bug #69024 (imagescale segfault with palette based image). (cmb)
  . Fixed bug #53154 (Zero-height rectangle has whiskers). (cmb)
  . Fixed bug #67447 (imagecrop() add a black line when cropping). (cmb)
  . Fixed bug #68714 (copy 'n paste error). (cmb)
  . Fixed bug #66339 (PHP segfaults in imagexbm). (cmb)
  . Fixed bug #70047 (gd_info() doesn't report WebP support). (cmb)
  . Replace libvpx with libwebp for bundled libgd. (cmb, Anatol)
  . Fixed bug #61221 (imagegammacorrect function loses alpha channel). (cmb)
  . Made fontFetch's path parser thread-safe. (Sara)
  . Removed T1Lib support. (Kalle)

- GMP:
  . Fixed bug #70284 (Use after free vulnerability in unserialize() with GMP).
      (stas)

- hash:
  . Fixed bug #70312 (HAVAL gives wrong hashes in specific cases). (letsgolee
      at naver dot com)

- IMAP:
  . Fixed bug #70158 (Building with static imap fails). (cmb)
  . Fixed bug #69998 (curl multi leaking memory). (Pierrick)

- Intl:

  . Fixed bug #70453 (IntlChar::foldCase() incorrect arguments and missing
      constants). (cmb)
  . Fixed bug #70454 (IntlChar::forDigit second parameter should be optional).
      (cmb, colinodell)
  . Removed deprecated aliases datefmt_set_timezone_id() and
      IntlDateFormatter::setTimeZoneID(). (Nikita)

- JSON:
  . Fixed bug #62010 (json_decode produces invalid byte-sequences).
      (Jakub Zelenka)
  . Fixed bug #68546 (json_decode() Fatal error: Cannot access property
      started with '\0'). (Jakub Zelenka)
  . Replace non-free JSON parser with a parser from Jsond extension, fixes #63520
      (JSON extension includes a problematic license statement). (Jakub Zelenka)
  . Fixed bug #68938 (json_decode() decodes empty string without error).
      (jeremy at bat-country dot us)

- LDAP:
  . Fixed bug #47222 (Implement LDAP_OPT_DIAGNOSTIC_MESSAGE). (Andreas Heigl)

- LiteSpeed:
  . Updated LiteSpeed SAPI code from V5.5 to V6.6. (George Wang)

- libxml:
  . Fixed handling of big lines in error messages with libxml >= 2.9.0.
      (Christoph M. Becker)

- Mcrypt:
  . Fixed bug #70625 (mcrypt_encrypt() won't return data when no IV was
      specified under RC4). (Nikita)
  . Fixed bug #69833 (mcrypt fd caching not working). (Anatol)
  . Fixed possible read after end of buffer and use after free. (Dmitry)
  . Removed mcrypt_generic_end() alias. (Nikita)
  . Removed mcrypt_ecb(), mcrypt_cbc(), mcrypt_cfb(), mcrypt_ofb(). (Nikita)

- Mysqli:
  . Fixed bug #32490 (constructor of mysqli has wrong name). (cmb)

- Mysqlnd:
  . Fixed bug #70949 (SQL Result Sets With NULL Can Cause Fatal Memory Errors).
      (Laruence)
  . Fixed bug #70384 (mysqli_real_query():Unknown type 245 sent by the server).
      (Andrey)
  . Fixed bug #70456 (mysqlnd doesn't activate TCP keep-alive when connecting to
      a server). (Sergei Turchanov)
  . Fixed bug #70572 segfault in mysqlnd_connect. (Andrey, Remi)
  . Fixed Bug #69796 (mysqli_stmt::fetch doesn't assign null values to
      bound variables). (Laruence)

- OCI8:

54

. Fixed memory leak with LOBs. (Senthil)
. Fixed bug #68298 (OCI int overflow) (Senthil).
. Corrected oci8 hash destructors to prevent segfaults, and a few other fixes.
  (Cameron Porter)

- ODBC:
. Fixed bug #69975 (PHP segfaults when accessing nvarchar(max) defined
  columns). (cmb)

- Opcache:
. Fixed bug #70656 (require() statement broken after opcache_reset() or a
  few hours of use). (Laruence)
. Fixed bug #70843 (Segmentation fault on MacOSX with
  opcache.file_cache_only=1). (Laruence)
. Fixed bug #70724 (Undefined Symbols from opcache.so on Mac OS X 10.10).
  (Laruence)
. Fixed compatibility with Windows 10 (see also bug #70652). (Anatol)
. Attmpt to fix "Unable to reattach to base address" problem. (Matt Ficken)
. Fixed bug #70423 (Warning Internal error: wrong size calculation). (Anatol)
. Fixed bug #70237 (Empty while and do-while segmentation fault with opcode
  on CLI enabled). (Dmitry, Laruence)
. Fixed bug #70111 (Segfault when a function uses both an explicit return
  type and an explicit cast). (Laruence)
. Fixed bug #70058 (Build fails when building for i386). (Laruence)
. Fixed bug #70022 (Crash with opcache using opcache.file_cache_only=1).
  (Anatol)
. Removed opcache.load_comments configuration directive. Now doc comments
  loading costs nothing and always enabled.
  (Dmitry)
. Fixed bug #69838 (Wrong size calculation for function table). (Anatol)
. Fixed bug #69688 (segfault with eval and opcache fast shutdown).
  (Laruence)
. Added experimental (disabled by default) file based opcode cache.
  (Dmitry, Laruence, Anatol)
. Fixed bug with try blocks being removed when extended_info opcode
  generation is turned on. (Laruence)
. Fixed bug #68644 (strlen incorrect : mbstring + func_overload=2 +UTF-8
  + Opcache). (Laruence)

- OpenSSL:
. Require at least OpenSSL version 0.9.8. (Jakub Zelenka)
. Fixed bug #68312 (Lookup for openssl.cnf causes a message box). (Anatol)
. Fixed bug #55259 (openssl extension does not get the DH parameters from
  DH key resource). (Jakub Zelenka)
. Fixed bug #70395 (Missing ARG_INFO for openssl_seal()). (cmb)
. Fixed bug #60632 (openssl_seal fails with AES). (Jakub Zelenka)
. Implemented FR #70438 (Add IV parameter for openssl_seal and openssl_open)
  (Jakub Zelenka)
. Fixed bug #70014

(openssl_random_pseudo_bytes() is not cryptographically
  secure). (Stas)
. Fixed bug #69882 (OpenSSL error "key values mismatch" after
  openssl_pkcs12_read with extra cert). (Tomasz Sawicki)
. Added "alpn_protocols" SSL context option allowing encrypted client/server
  streams to negotiate alternative protocols using the ALPN TLS extension when
  built against OpenSSL 1.0.2 or newer. Negotiated protocol information is
  accessible through stream_get_meta_data() output.
. Removed "CN_match" and "SNI_server_name" SSL context options. Use automatic
  detection or the "peer_name" option instead. (Nikita)

- Pcntl:
. Fixed bug #70386 (Can't compile on NetBSD because of missing WCONTINUED
  and WIFCONTINUED). (Matteo)
. Fixed bug #60509 (pcntl_signal doesn't decrease ref-count of old handler
  when setting SIG_DFL). (Julien)
. Implemented FR #68505 (Added wifcontinued and wcontinued). (xilon-jul)
. Added rusage support to pcntl_wait() and pcntl_waitpid(). (Anton Stepanenko,
  Tony)

- PCRE:
. Fixed bug #70232 (Incorrect bump-along behavior with \K and empty string
  match). (cmb)
. Fixed bug #70345 (Multiple vulnerabilities related to PCRE functions).
  (Anatol Belski)
. Fixed bug #70232 (Incorrect bump-along behavior with \K and empty string
  match). (cmb)
. Fixed bug #53823 (preg_replace: * qualifier on unicode replace garbles the
  string). (cmb)
. Fixed bug #69864 (Segfault in preg_replace_callback). (cmb, ab)

- PDO:
. Fixed bug #70861 (Segmentation fault in pdo_parse_params() during Drupal 8
  test suite). (Anatol)
. Fixed bug #70389 (PDO constructor changes unrelated variables). (Laruence)
. Fixed bug #70272 (Segfault in pdo_mysql). (Laruence)
. Fixed bug #70221 (persistent sqlite connection + custom function
  segfaults). (Laruence)
. Removed support for the /e (PREG_REPLACE_EVAL) modifier. (Nikita)
. Fixed bug #59450 (./configure fails with "Cannot find php_pdo_driver.h").
  (maxime dot besson at smile dot fr)

- PDO_DBlib:
. Fixed bug #69757 (Segmentation fault on nextRowset).
  (miracle at rpz dot name)

- PDO_mysql:
. Fixed bug #68424 (Add new PDO mysql

55

connection attr to control multi
    statements option). (peter dot wolanin at
acquia dot com)

- PDO_OCI:
    . Fixed bug #70308 (PDO::ATTR_PREFETCH is
ignored). (Chris Jones)

- PDO_pgsql:
    . Fixed bug #69752 (PDOStatement::execute()
leaks memory with DML
    Statements when closeCuror() is u). (Philip
Hofstetter)
    . Removed
PGSQL_ATTR_DISABLE_NATIVE_PREPARED_STAT
EMENT attribute in favor of
    ATTR_EMULATE_PREPARES). (Nikita)

- Phar:
    . Fixed bug #69720 (Null pointer dereference in
phar_get_fp_offset()). (Stas)
    . FIxed bug #70433 (Uninitialized pointer in
phar_make_dirstream when zip
    entry filename is "/"). (Stas)
    . Improved fix for bug #69441. (Anatol Belski)
    . Fixed bug #70019 (Files extracted from archive
may be placed outside of
    destination directory). (Anatol Belski)

- Phpdbg:
    . Fixed bug #70614 (incorrect exit code in -rr
mode with Exceptions). (Bob)
    . Fixed bug #70532 (phpdbg must respect
set_exception_handler). (Bob)
    . Fixed bug #70531 (Run and quit mode (-qrr)
should not fallback to
    interactive mode). (Bob)
    . Fixed bug #70533 (Help overview (-h) does not
rpint anything under Windows).
    (Anatol)
    . Fixed bug #70449 (PHP won't compile on 10.4
and 10.5 because of missing
    constants). (Bob)
    . Fixed bug #70214 (FASYNC not defined, needs
sys/file.h include). (Bob)
    . Fixed bug #70138 (Segfault when displaying
memory leaks). (Bob)

- Reflection:
    . Fixed bug #70650 (Wrong docblock
assignment). (Marcio)
    . Fixed bug #70674
(ReflectionFunction::getClosure() leaks memory
when used
    for internal functions). (Dmitry, Bob)
    . Fixed bug causing bogus traces for
ReflectionGenerator::getTrace(). (Bob)
    . Fixed inheritance chain of Reflector interface.
(Tjerk)
    . Added ReflectionGenerator class. (Bob)
    . Added reflection support for return types and
type declarations. (Sara,
    Matteo)

- Session:
    . Fixed bug #70876 (Segmentation fault when
regenerating session id with
    strict mode). (Laruence)
    . Fixed bug #70529 (Session read causes "String
is not zero-terminated" error).
    (Yasuo)
    . Fixed bug #70013 (Reference to $_SESSION is
lost after a call to

session_regenerate_id()). (Yasuo)
    . Fixed bug #69952 (Data integrity issues
accessing superglobals by
    reference). (Bob)
    . Fixed bug #67694 (Regression in
session_regenerate_id()). (Tjerk)
    . Fixed bug #68941 (mod_files.sh is a bash-
script). (bugzilla at ii.nl, Yasuo)

- SOAP:
    . Fixed bug #70940 (Segfault in soap /
type_to_string). (Remi)
    . Fixed bug #70900 (SoapClient systematic out
of memory error). (Dmitry)
    . Fixed bug #70875 (Segmentation fault if wsdl
has no targetNamespace
    attribute). (Matteo)
    . Fixed bug #70715 (Segmentation fault inside
soap client). (Laruence)
    . Fixed bug #70709 (SOAP Client generates
Segfault). (Laruence)
    . Fixed bug #70388 (SOAP
serialize_function_call() type confusion / RCE).
    (Stas)
    . Fixed bug #70081 (SoapClient info leak / null
pointer dereference via
    multiple type confusions). (Stas)
    . Fixed bug #70079 (Segmentation fault after
more than 100 SoapClient
    calls). (Laruence)
    . Fixed bug #70032 (make_http_soap_request
calls
    zend_hash_get_current_key_ex(,,,NULL).
(Laruence)
    . Fixed bug #68361 (Segmentation fault on
SoapClient::__getTypes). (Laruence)

- SPL:
    . Fixed bug #70959 (ArrayObject unserialize
does not restore protected
    fields). (Laruence)
    . Fixed bug #70853 (SplFixedArray throws
exception when using ref variable
    as index). (Laruence)
    . Fixed bug #70868 (PCRE JIT and pattern reuse
segfault). (Laruence)
    . Fixed bug #70730 (Incorrect ArrayObject
serialization if unset is called
    in serialize()). (Laruence)
    . Fixed bug #70573 (Cloning SplPriorityQueue
leads to memory leaks). (Dmitry)
    . Fixed bug #70303 (Incorrect constructor
reflection for ArrayObject). (cmb)
    . Fixed bug #70068 (Dangling pointer in the
unserialization of ArrayObject
    items). (sean.heelan)
    . Fixed bug #70166 (Use After Free Vulnerability
in unserialize() with
    SPLArrayObject). (taoguangchen at icloud dot
com)
    . Fixed bug #70168 (Use After Free Vulnerability
in unserialize() with
    SplObjectStorage). (taoguangchen at icloud dot
com)
    . Fixed bug #70169 (Use After Free Vulnerability
in unserialize() with
    SplDoublyLinkedList). (taoguangchen at icloud
dot com)
    . Fixed bug #70053 (MutlitpleIterator array-keys
incompatible change in
    PHP 7). (Tjerk)
    . Fixed bug #69970 (Use-after-free vulnerability
in

spl_recursive_it_move_forward_ex()).
(Laruence)
. Fixed bug #69845 (ArrayObject with
ARRAY_AS_PROPS broken). (Dmitry)
. Changed ArrayIterator implementation using
zend_hash_iterator_... API.
   Allowed modification of iterated ArrayObject
using the same behavior
   as proposed in `Fix "foreach" behavior`.
Removed "Array was modified
   outside object and internal position is no longer
valid" hack. (Dmitry)
. Implemented FR #67886
(SplPriorityQueue/SplHeap doesn't expose
extractFlags
   nor curruption state). (Julien)
. Fixed bug #66405
(RecursiveDirectoryIterator::CURRENT_AS_PATHN
AME
   breaks the RecursiveIterator). (Paul Garvin)

- SQLite3:
. Fixed bug #70571 (Memory leak in
sqlite3_do_callback). (Adam)
. Fixed bug #69972 (Use-after-free vulnerability
in
   sqlite3SafetyCheckSickOrOk()). (Laruence)
. Fixed bug #69897 (segfault when manually
constructing SQLite3Result).
   (Kalle)
. Fixed bug #68260 (SQLite3Result::fetchArray
declares wrong
   required_num_args). (Julien)

- Standard:
. Fixed count on symbol tables. (Laruence)
. Fixed bug #70963 (Unserialize shows
UNKNOWN in result). (Laruence)
. Fixed bug #70910 (extract() breaks variable
references). (Laruence)
. Fixed bug #70808 (array_merge_recursive
corrupts memory of unset items).
   (Laruence)
. Fixed bug #70667 (strtr() causes invalid writes
and a crashes). (Dmitry)
. Fixed bug #70668 (array_keys() doesn't
respect references when $strict is
   true). (Bob, Dmitry)
. Implemented the RFC `Random Functions
Throwing Exceptions in PHP 7`.
   (Sammy Kaye Powers, Anthony)
. Fixed bug #70487 (pack('x') produces an
error). (Nikita)
. Fixed bug #70342 (changing configuration with
ignore_user_abort(true) isn't
   working). (Laruence)
. Fixed bug #70295 (Segmentation fault with
setrawcookie). (Bob)
. Fixed bug #67131 (setcookie() conditional for
empty values not met). (cmb)
. Fixed bug #70365 (Use-after-free vulnerability
in unserialize() with
   SplObjectStorage). (taoguangchen at icloud dot
com)
. Fixed bug #70366 (Use-after-free vulnerability
in unserialize() with
   SplDoublyLinkedList). (taoguangchen at icloud
dot com)
. Fixed bug #70250 (extract() turns array
elements to references).
   (Laruence)
. Fixed bug #70211 (php 7
ZEND_HASH_IF_FULL_DO_RESIZE use after free).

(Laruence)
. Fixed bug #70208 (Assert breaking access on
objects). (Bob)
. Fixed bug #70140
(str_ireplace/php_string_tolower - Arbitrary Code
   Execution). (CVE-2015-6527) (Laruence)
. Implemented FR #70112 (Allow "dirname" to
go up various times). (Remi)
. Fixed bug #36365 (scandir duplicates file name
at every 65535th file). (cmb)
. Fixed bug #70096 (Repeated iptcembed() adds
superfluous FF bytes). (cmb)
. Fixed bug #70018 (exec does not strip all
whitespace). (Laruence)
. Fixed bug #69983 (get_browser fails with user
agent of null).
   (Kalle, cmb, Laruence)
. Fixed bug #69976 (Unable to parse "all" urls
with colon char). (cmb)
. Fixed bug #69768 (escapeshell*() doesn't cater
to !). (cmb)
. Fixed bug #62922 (Truncating entire string
should result in string).
   (Nikita)
. Fixed bug #69723 (Passing parameters by
reference and array_column).
   (Laruence)
. Fixed bug #69523 (Cookie name cannot be
empty). (Christoph M. Becker)
. Fixed bug #69325 (php_copy_file_ex does not
pass the argument).
   (imbolk at gmail dot com)
. Fixed bug #69299 (Regression in array_filter's
$flag argument in PHP 7).
   (Laruence)
. Removed call_user_method() and
call_user_method_array() functions. (Kalle)
. Fixed user session handlers (See
rfc:session.user.return-value). (Sara)
. Added intdiv() function. (Andrea)
. Improved precision of log() function for base 2
and 10. (Marc Bennewitz)
. Remove string category support in setlocale().
(Nikita)
. Remove set_magic_quotes_runtime() and its
alias magic_quotes_runtime().
   (Nikita)
. Fixed bug #65272 (flock() out parameter not
set correctly in windows).
   (Daniel Lowrey)
. Added preg_replace_callback_array function.
(Wei Dai)
. Deprecated salt option to password_hash.
(Anthony)
. Fixed bug #69686 (password_verify reports
back error on PHP7 will null
   string). (Anthony)
. Added Windows support for getrusage(). (Kalle)
. Removed hardcoded limit on number of pipes in
proc_open(). (Tony)

- Streams:
. Fixed bug #70361 (HTTP stream wrapper
doesn't close keep-alive connections).
   (Niklas Keller)
. Fixed bug #68532 (convert.base64-encode
omits padding bytes).
   (blaesius at krumedia dot de)
. Removed set_socket_blocking() in favor of its
alias stream_set_blocking().
   (Nikita)

- Tokenizer:

. Fixed bug #69430 (token_get_all has new irrecoverable errors). (Nikita)

- XMLReader:
. Fixed bug #70309 (XmlReader read generates extra output). (Anatol)

- XMLRPC
. Fixed bug #70526 (xmlrpc_set_type returns false on success). (Laruence)

- XSL:
. Fixed bug #70678 (PHP7 returns true when false is expected). (Felipe)
. Fixed bug #70535 (XSLT: free(): invalid pointer). (Laruence)
. Fixed bug #69782 (NULL pointer dereference). (Stas)
. Fixed bug #64776 (The XSLT extension is not thread safe). (Mike)
. Removed xsl.security_prefs ini option. (Nikita)

- Zlib:
. Added deflate_init(), deflate_add(), inflate_init(), inflate_add() functions allowing incremental/streaming compression/decompression.
(Daniel Lowrey & Bob Weinand)

- Zip:
. Fixed bug #70322 (ZipArchive::close() doesn't indicate errors). (cmb)
. Fixed bug #70350 (ZipArchive::extractTo allows for directory traversal when
creating directories). (neal at fb dot com)
. Added ZipArchive::setCompressionName and ZipArchive::setCompressionIndex
methods. (Remi, Cedric Delmas)
. Update bundled libzip to 1.0.1. (Remi, Anatol)
. Fixed bug #67161 (ZipArchive::getStream() returns NULL for certain file).
(Christoph M. Becker)

CHAPTER 4.
PHP 7.1

In this chapter, we will look at some of the awesome features introduced in PHP 7.1. This includes more array and closure features, new scalar types for defining NULLs and returning them by VOIDs. Additionally, we will see new hashing functions and catching multiple exceptions.

4.1. New Functionality

4.1.1. Iterables

Iterable is a new pseudo-type introduced in the second stable PHP 7 version. The main advantage of having iterable is that a class, method or function parameter can be declared iterable, without being concerned about the implementation (for example: `array`, `Iterator`, `Generator`, etc). So anything that is iterable will inherit that pseudo-type.

```
Example
function example(iterable $iterable = []) {
    // ...
}

Example
function example(): iterable {
    return [a, b, c];
}
```

4.1.2. Closure::fromCallable

The Closure class has now a new static `fromCallable()` method, which automatically creates a `Closure` from any callbable you pass to it.

```
public static Closure Closure::fromCallable ( callable $callable )
```

```
Example
$data = collection([1,2,3,4]);
$integers = $data>test(Closure::fromCallable('is_float'));
```

4.1.3. Symmetric array destructuring

The shorthand array syntax (`[]`) may now be used to restructure arrays in assignments (including within `foreach`), as an alternative to the existing `list()` syntax, which is still supported.

```
Example
[$name, $email] = ["Joe", "j@doe.pl"];
```

4.1.4. hash_hkdf()

A `hash_hkdf()` function generates a HKDF key derivation of a supplied key input.

```
string hash_hkdf ( string $algo , string $ikm [, int $length = 0 [, string $info = " [,
string $salt = " ]]] )
```

Returns a string of derived key in a raw binary representation.

4.1.5. Nullable Types

This feature adds a leading question mark symbol (?) to indicate that a type can also be `null`. Nullable types can be formed from any currently permitted type. Nullable types are permitted anywhere type declarations with only limitation to some inheritance rules. The syntax chosen is the same used by Hack, where a question mark is used to prefix a type to denote it as nullable.

```
function foo(): ?int {
    return null; //ok
}

function foo(): ?int {
    return 42; // ok
}

function foo(): ?int {
    return 'test'; // error
}
```

4.1.6. [] = as alternative construct to list()

From PHP version 7.1 you can specify keys in `list()`, or its new shorthand `[]` syntax. This enables restructuring of arrays with non-integer or non-sequential keys. This pattern matching ability also enables for values to be more easily extracted from arrays.

```
$data = [
    ["id" => 1, "name" => 'Tom'],
    ["id" => 2, "name" => 'Fred'],
];

// list() style
list("id" => $id1, "name" => $name1) = $data[0];

// [] style
["id" => $id1, "name" => $name1] = $data[0];
```

4.1.7. Void return type

We can now specify a null type of returned value from a function. Sometimes we may want to specify the function which should not return any value to the user. Functions declared with `void` as their return type can either omit their return statement altogether, or use an empty return statement. null is not a valid return value for a void function. Attempting to use a void function's return value simply evaluates to NULL, with no warnings emitted.

```php
function should_return_nothing(): void {
    return 1; // Fatal error: A void function must not return a value
}

function returns_null(): void {
    return null; // Fatal error: A void function must not return a value
}
function lacks_return(): void {
    // valid
}
function returns_nothing(): void {
    return; // valid
}
```

4.1.8. Catching Multiple Exception Types

To save some code logic, we can finally determine many different types to be caught in a single `catch()` definition. This is useful when similar exceptions should be handled in the same way.

```php
try {
    // Some code...
} catch (ExceptionType1 | ExceptionType2 $e) {
    // Code to handle the exception
} catch (\Exception $e) {
    // ...
}
```

4.1.9. Too few arguments to function

In PHP 7.1, calling a function without required parameters will trigger an Error exception, `ArgumentCountError`.

```php
function sayHello($name) {
    echo "Hello " . $name;
}
sayHello();
// Fatal error: Uncaught ArgumentCountError: Too few arguments to function
sayHello(), 0 passed in...
```

4.1.10. SHA512/256 & SHA512/224

There have been added two new hashing algorithms: `SHA512/256` and `SHA512/224` to the global list.

```
$hashed = hash('sha512', $data);
```

4.1.11. is_iterable

A new function is here to verify that the contents of a variable is an iterable value.

```
bool is_iterable ( mixed $var )
```

4.1.12. socket_export_stream

A new `socket_export_stream()` function exports a socket extension resource into a stream that encapsulates a socket.

```
resource socket_export_stream ( resource $socket )
```

4.2. Fixed bugs

#76025. It is now available to throw any custom exceptions within the function registered under `set_error_handler()`. Previously the following case would return Segmentation fault:

```
function handleError($errno, $errstr, $errfile, $errline) {
    throw new Exception("custom exception message");
}
set_error_handler('handleError', E_ALL);

$a = $somethingNasty[$b];
//will output
Exception thrown with message: custom exception message
```

#74408. Endless loop is caused by calling missing class within the `set_error_handler()` function, which even bypass the PHP execution time limit. This bug has caused some unwanted gate to potential DoS attacks as the execution time is endless and will never be killed by the server.

```
class ErrorHandling {

    public function error_handler(int $errno, string $errstr, string $errfile, int $errline):
    void {
        new NonExistingCustomClass();
    }

    public function exception_handler(Throwable $e): void { }

}

set_error_handler('ErrorHandling::error_handler');
set_exception_handler('ErrorHandling::exception_handler');

new InvalidClassName();
//will now throw the exception of not found class
```

#75946. `session_start()` would fail after `fastcgi_finish_⤶ request()` is called in the same file, causing the session function to always return FALSE.

```
session_start();

echo session_id()."\n";
$_SESSION['test'] = 1;

echo "stop session\n";
session_write_close();

fastcgi_finish_request();

session_start();
$_SESSION['test'] = 2;
session_write_close();


$status = session_start();
```

// $start will now produce the TRUE result

#75781. `substr_count()` display incorrect results for big string objects, larger than 4GB as a result.

```
$size = 9*1024*1024*1024;
$buf = str_repeat(chr(0),$size);

for( $i=0; $i < $size; $i++ ) {
   if( $i % 3 == 0 ) {
      $buf{$i}=chr(255);
   }
}
$cnt=substr_count($buf,chr(255));
var_dump($cnt);

//PHP 7.1
----------------
int(3221225472)

//pre PHP 7.1
--------------
int(-1073741824)
```

#75775. `readline_read_history()` no longer returns segmentation fault for empty files, now it will output the history, so nothing really as there isn't any content inside:

```
touch("empty.file");
readline_read_history("empty.file");
//this works fine and will not return anything
```

#75675. Fatal error is no longer thrown together with Exception when we create an instance of `SoapClient` with non-existing URL address. The class will only throw the related Exception about the issue with the location provided.

```
set_error_handler(function() {
```

```
    echo 'error'.PHP_EOL;
}, E_ALL);

try {
    $client = new SoapClient('http://nonExistingAddress, ['exceptions' => true, 'trace'
=> 0]);
} catch (SoapFault $exception) {
    var_dump('Exception: '.$exception->getMessage());
} catch (Exception $exception) {
    var_dump('Exception: '.$exception->getMessage());
}
```

```
//current behavior
error
string(143) "Exception: SOAP-ERROR: Parsing WSDL: Couldn't load from
'thisaddressdoesnotexists' : failed to load external entity "thisaddressdoesnotexists"
```

```
//previous behavior
error
PHP Fatal error:  SOAP-ERROR: Parsing WSDL: Couldn't load from
'thisaddressdoesnotexists' : failed to load external entity "thisaddressdoesnotexists"
 in C:\Users\.....\soaptest.php on line 9
string(143) "Exception: SOAP-ERROR: Parsing WSDL: Couldn't load from
'thisaddressdoesnotexists' : failed to load external entity "thisaddressdoesnotexists"
```

#74606. Nesting a `try/finally` block inside of `try/catch` within a loop with `Generator` inside will no longer cause too many live variables to be cleaned up, so it will avoid another segmentation fault returned by the following:

```
function gen() {
    $array = ["foo"];
    $array[] = "bar";

    foreach ($array as $item) {
        try {
            try {
                yield;
            } finally {
                echo "fin $item\n";
            }
        } catch (\Exception $e) {
```

```
            echo "catch\n";
            continue;
        }
    }
}
$g = gen();
$g->throw(new Exception);

//PHP 7.1
fin foo
catch
fin bar

//pre PHP 7.1
fin foo
catch
fin bar
<segmentation fault>
```

#74589. `__DIR__` was not returning the correct location if the location is ending with non-standard character, like for instance unicode character. For example this does not break anymore:

```
//file saved to: D:\someFolderÓ\test.php
echo __DIR__, "\n";
echo dirname(__FILE__), "\n";
var_dump(__DIR__ === dirname(__FILE__));

//will output:
D:\
D:\someFolderÓ\
bool(false)
```

#74318. Partially uploaded files haven't been deleted before from the `upload_temp_dir`, because the garbage collector still thinks that a file is still in upload phase.

#73113. Objects which throws exceptions are causing segmentation fault when trying to `jsonSerialize()` it via `json_encode()`.

```
class JsonSerializableObject implements \JsonSerializable
{
    public function jsonSerialize()
    {
        throw new \Exception('This error will be called when json_ecode is used');
    }
}

$obj = new JsonSerializableObject();

json_encode($obj);
//this will now finally thrown an exception
```

4.3. Deprecated elements

4.3.1. ext/mcrypt

The mcrypt extension has been removed and replaced by `OpenSSL`.

4.3.2. Eval option for mb_ereg_replace() and mb_eregi_replace()

Option "e" (`val()` resulting code) was removed from `mb_regex_set↪ _options`.

4.4. Change log

16 Aug 2018, PHP 7.1.21

- Calendar:
  . Fixed bug #52974 (jewish.c: compile error under Windows with GBK charset).
    (cmb)

- Filter:
  . Fixed bug #76366 (References in sub-array for filtering breaks the filter).
    (ZiHang Gao)

- PDO_Firebird:
  . Fixed bug #76488 (Memory leak when fetching

a BLOB field). (Simonov Denis)

- PDO_PgSQL:
  . Fixed bug #75402 (Possible Memory Leak using PDO::CURSOR_SCROLL option).
    (Anatol)

- SQLite3:
  . Fixed #76665 (SQLite3Stmt::bindValue() with SQLITE3_FLOAT doesn't juggle).
    (cmb)

- Standard:
  . Fixed bug #68553 (array_column: null values in

$index_key become incrementing
    keys in result). (Laruence)
  . Fixed bug #73817 (Incorrect entries in
get_html_translation_table). (cmb)
  . Fixed bug #76643 (Segmentation fault when
using `output_add_rewrite_var`).
    (cmb)

- Zip:
  . Fixed bug #76524 (ZipArchive memory leak
(OVERWRITE flag and empty archive)).
    (Timur Ibragimov)

07 Jul 2018, PHP 7.1.20

- Core:
  . Fixed bug #76534 (PHP hangs on 'illegal string
offset on string references
    with an error handler). (Laruence)
  . Fixed bug #76502 (Chain of mixed exceptions
and errors does not serialize
    properly). (Nikita)

- Date:
  . Fixed bug #76462 (Undefined property:
DateInterval::$f). (Anatol)

- FPM:
  . Fixed bug #73342 (Vulnerability in php-fpm by
changing stdin to
    non-blocking). (Nikita)

- GMP:
  . Fixed bug #74670 (Integer Underflow when
unserializing GMP and possible
    other classes). (Nikita)

- intl:
  . Fixed bug #76556 (get_debug_info handler for
BreakIterator shows wrong
    type). (cmb)

- mbstring:
  . Fixed bug #76532 (Integer overflow and
excessive memory usage
    in mb_strimwidth). (MarcusSchwarz)

- PGSQL:
  . Fixed bug #76548 (pg_fetch_result did not
fetch the next row). (Anatol)

- phpdbg:
  . Fix arginfo wrt. optional/required parameters.
(cmb)

- Reflection:
  . Fixed bug #76536 (PHP crashes with core dump
when throwing exception in
    error handler). (Laruence)
  . Fixed bug #75231
(ReflectionProperty#getValue() incorrectly works
with
    inherited classes). (Nikita)

- Standard:
  . Fixed bug #76505 (array_merge_recursive() is
duplicating sub-array keys).
    (Laruence)
  . Fixed bug #71848 (getimagesize with
$imageinfo returns false). (cmb)

22 Jun 2018, PHP 7.1.19

- CLI Server:
  . Fixed bug #76333 (PHP built-in server does not
find files if root path
    contains special characters). (Anatol)

- OpenSSL:
  . Fixed bug #76296 (openssl_pkey_get_public
does not respect open_basedir).
    (Erik Lax, Jakub Zelenka)
  . Fixed bug #76174 (openssl extension fails to
build with LibreSSL 2.7).
    (Jakub Zelenka)

- SPL:
  . Fixed bug #76367 (NoRewindIterator segfault
11). (Laruence)

- Standard:
  . Fixed bug #76335 ("link(): Bad file descriptor"
with non-ASCII path).
    (Anatol)
  . Fixed bug #76383 (array_map on $GLOBALS
returns IS_INDIRECT). (Bob)

24 May 2018, PHP 7.1.18

- FPM:
  . Fixed bug #76075 --with-fpm-acl wrongly tries
to find libacl on FreeBSD.
    (mgorny)

- intl:
  . Fixed bug #74385 (Locale::parseLocale()
broken with some arguments).
    (Anatol)

- Opcache:
  . Fixed bug #76205 (PHP-FPM sporadic crash
when running Infinitewp). (Dmitry)
  . Fixed bug #76275 (Assertion failure in file
cache when unserializing empty
    try_catch_array). (Nikita)
  . Fixed bug #76281 (Opcache causes incorrect
"undefined variable" errors).
    (Nikita)

- Reflection:
  . Fixed arginfo for array_replace(_recursive) and
array_merge(_recursive).
    (carusogabriel)

26 Apr 2018, PHP 7.1.17

- Date:
  . Fixed bug #76131 (mismatch arginfo for
date_create). (carusogabriel)

- FPM:
  . Fixed bug #68440 (ERROR: failed to reload:
execvp() failed: Argument list
    too long). (Jacob Hipps)
  . Fixed incorrect write to getenv result in FPM
reload. (Jakub Zelenka)

- GD:
  . Fixed bug #52070 (imagedashedline() - dashed
line sometimes is not visible).
    (cmb)

- intl:
  . Fixed bug #76153 (Intl compilation fails with
icu4c 61.1). (Anatol)

- mbstring:
  . Fixed bug #75944 (Wrong cp1251 detection). (dmk001)
  . Fixed bug #76113 (mbstring does not build with Oniguruma 6.8.1).
    (chrullrich, cmb)

- phpdbg:
  . Fixed bug #76143 (Memory corruption: arbitrary NUL overwrite). (Laurence)

- SPL:
  . Fixed bug #76131 (mismatch arginfo for splarray constructor).
    (carusogabriel)

- standard:
  . Fixed bug #75996 (incorrect url in header for mt_rand). (tatarbj)

29 Mar 2018, PHP 7.1.16

- Core:
  . Fixed bug #76025 (Segfault while throwing exception in error_handler).
    (Dmitry, Laurence)
  . Fixed bug #76044 ('date: illegal option -- -' in ./configure on FreeBSD).
    (Anatol)

- FPM:
  . Fixed bug #75605 (Dumpable FPM child processes allow bypassing opcache
    access controls). (Jakub Zelenka)

- GD:
  . Fixed bug #73957 (signed integer conversion in imagescale()). (cmb)

- ODBC:
  . Fixed bug #76088 (ODBC functions are not available by default on Windows).
    (cmb)

- Opcache:
  . Fixed bug #76074 (opcache corrupts variable in for-loop). (Bob)

- Phar:
  . Fixed bug #76085 (Segmentation fault in buildFromIterator when directory
    name contains a \n). (Laurence)

- Standard:
  . Fixed bug #74139 (mail.add_x_header default inconsistent with docs). (cmb)
  . Fixed bug #76068 (parse_ini_string fails to parse "[foo]\nbar=1|>baz" with
    segfault). (Anatol)

01 Mar 2018, PHP 7.1.15

- Apache2Handler:
  . Fixed bug #75882 (a simple way for segfaults in threadsafe php just with
    configuration). (Anatol)

- Date:
  . Fixed bug #75857 (Timezone gets truncated when formatted). (carusogabriel)
  . Fixed bug #75928 (Argument 2 for `DateTimeZone::listIdentifiers()` should

accept `null`). (Pedro Lacerda)
  . Fixed bug #68406 (calling var_dump on a DateTimeZone object modifies it).
    (jhdxr)

- FTP:
  . Fixed ftp_pasv arginfo. (carusogabriel)

-GD:
  . Fixed imagesetinterpolation arginfo. (Gabriel Caruso)

- iconv:
  . Fixed bug #75867 (Freeing uninitialized pointer). (Philip Prindeville)

- LDAP:
  . Fixed bug #49876 (Fix LDAP path lookup on 64-bit distros). (dzuelke)

- libxml2:
  . Fixed bug #75871 (use pkg-config where available). (pmmaga)

- mysqlnd:
  . Fixed negotiation of MySQL authenticaton plugin. (Johannes)
  . Fixed a memleak with SSL connections. (Johannes)

- ODBC:
  . Fixed bug #73725 (Unable to retrieve value of varchar(max) type). (Anatol)

- Opcache:
  . Fixed bug #75969 (Assertion failure in live range DCE due to block pass
    misoptimization). (Nikita)

- OpenSSL:
  . Fixed openssl_* arginfos. (carusogabriel)

- PCNTL:
  . Fixed bug #75873 (pcntl_wexitstatus returns incorrect on Big_Endian platform
    (s390x)). (Sam Ding)

- PGSQL:
  . Fixed #75838 (Memory leak in pg_escape_bytea()). (ard_1 at mail dot ru)

- Phar:
  . Fixed bug #65414 (deal with leading slash when adding files correctly).
    (bishopb)

- SPL:
  . Fixed bug #74519 (strange behavior of AppendIterator). (jhdxr)

- Standard:
  . Fixed bug #75961 (Strange references behavior). (Laurence)
  . Fixed bug #75916 (DNS_CAA record results contain garbage). (Mike,
    Philip Sharp)
  . Fixed some arginfos. (carusogabriel)
  . Fixed bug #75981 (stack-buffer-overflow while parsing HTTP response). (Stas)

01 Feb 2018, PHP 7.1.14

- Core:

. Fixed bug #75679 (Path 260 character problem). (Anatol)
. Fixed bug #75786 (segfault when using spread operator on generator passed
    by reference). (Nikita)
. Fixed bug #75799 (arg of get_defined_functions is optional). (carusogabriel)
. Fixed bug #75396 (Exit inside generator finally results in fatal error).
    (Nikita)
. Fixed bug #75079 (self keyword leads to incorrectly generated TypeError when
    in closure in trait). (Nikita)

- FCGI:
. Fixed bug #75794 (getenv() crashes on Windows 7.2.1 when second parameter is
    false). (Anatol)

- IMAP:
. Fixed bug #75774 (imap_append HeapCorruction). (Anatol)

- Mbstring:
. Fixed bug #62545 (wrong unicode mapping in some charsets). (cmb)

- Opcache:
. Fixed bug #75720 (File cache not populated after SHM runs full). (Dmitry)
. Fixed bug #75579 (Interned strings buffer overflow may cause crash).
    (Dmitry)

- PGSQL:
. Fixed bug #75671 (pg_version() crashes when called on a connection to
    cockroach). (magicaltux at gmail dot com)

- Readline:
. Fixed bug #75775 (readline_read_history segfaults with empty file).
    (Anatol)

- SAPI:
. Fixed bug #75735 ([embed SAPI] Segmentation fault in
    sapi_register_post_entry). (Laruence)

- SOAP:
. Fixed bug #70469 (SoapClient generates E_ERROR even if exceptions=1 is
    used). (Anton Artamonov)
. Fixed bug #75502 (Segmentation fault in zend_string_release). (Nikita)

- SPL:
. Fixed bug #75717 (RecursiveArrayIterator does not traverse arrays by
    reference). (Nikita)
. Fixed bug #75242 (RecursiveArrayIterator doesn't have constants from parent
    class). (Nikita)
. Fixed bug #73209 (RecursiveArrayIterator does not iterate object
    properties). (Nikita)

- Standard:
. Fixed bug #75781 (substr_count incorrect result). (Laruence)

04 Jan 2018, PHP 7.1.13

- Core:
. Fixed bug #75573 (Segmentation fault in 7.1.12 and 7.0.26). (Laruence)
. Fixed bug #75384 (PHP seems incompatible with OneDrive files on demand).
    (Anatol)
. Fixed bug #74862 (Unable to clone instance when private __clone defined).
    (Daniel Ciochiu)
. Fixed bug #75074 (php-process crash when is_file() is used with strings
    longer 260 chars). (Anatol)
. Fixed bug #69727 (Remove timestamps from build to make it reproducible).
    (Jelle van der Waa)

- CLI Server:
. Fixed bug #60471 (Random "Invalid request (unexpected EOF)" using a router
    script). (SammyK)
. Fixed bug #73830 (Directory does not exist). (Anatol)

- FPM:
. Fixed bug #64938 (libxml_disable_entity_loader setting is shared between
    requests). (Remi)

- GD:
. Fixed bug #75571 (Potential infinite loop in gdImageCreateFromGifCtx).
    (Christoph)

- Opcache:
. Fixed bug #75608 ("Narrowing occurred during type inference" error).
    (Laruence, Dmitry)
. Fixed bug #75570 ("Narrowing occurred during type inference" error).
    (Dmitry)
. Fixed bug #75579 (Interned strings buffer overflow may cause crash).
    (Dmitry)

- PCRE:
. Fixed bug #74183 (preg_last_error not returning error code after error).
    (Andrew Nester)

- Phar:
. Fixed bug #74782 (remove file name from output to avoid XSS). (stas)

- Standard:
. Fixed bug #75511 (fread not free unused buffer). (Laruence)
. Fixed bug #75514 (mt_rand returns value outside [$min,$max]+ on 32-bit)
    (Remi)
. Fixed bug #75535 (Inappropriately parsing HTTP response leads to PHP
    segment fault). (Nikita)
. Fixed bug #75409 (accept EFAULT in addition to ENOSYS as indicator
    that getrandom() is missing). (sarciszewski)
. Fixed bug #73124 (php_ini_scanned_files() not reporting correctly).
    (John Stevenson)
. Fixed bug #75574 (putenv does not work properly if parameter contains
    non-ASCII unicode character). (Anatol)

- Zip:
  . Fixed bug #75540 (Segfault with libzip 1.3.1). (Remi)

23 Nov 2017, PHP 7.1.12

- Core:
  . Fixed bug #75420 (Crash when modifing property name in __isset for
    BP_VAR_IS). (Laruence)
  . Fixed bug #75368 (mmap/munmap trashing on unlucky allocations). (Nikita,
    Dmitry)

- CLI:
  . Fixed bug #75287 (Builtin webserver crash after chdir in a shutdown
    function). (Laruence)

- Enchant:
  . Fixed bug #53070 (enchant_broker_get_path crashes if no path is set). (jelle
    van der Waa, cmb)
  . Fixed bug #75365 (Enchant still reports version 1.1.0). (cmb)

- Exif:
  . Fixed bug #75301 (Exif extension has built in revision version). (Peter
    Kokot)

- GD:
  . Fixed bug #65148 (imagerotate may alter image dimensions). (cmb)
  . Fixed bug #75437 (Wrong reflection on imagewebp). (Fabien Villepinte)

- intl:
  . Fixed bug #75317 (UConverter::setDestinationEncoding changes source instead
    of destination). (andrewnester)

- interbase:
  . Fixed bug #75453 (Incorrect reflection for ibase_[p]connect). (villfa)

- Mysqli:
  . Fixed bug #75434 (Wrong reflection for mysqli_fetch_all function). (Fabien
    Villepinte)

- OCI8:
  . Fixed valgrind issue. (Tianfang Yang)

- OpenSSL:
  . Fixed bug #75363 (openssl_x509_parse leaks memory). (Bob, Jakub Zelenka)
  . Fixed bug #75307 (Wrong reflection for openssl_open function). (villfa)

- Opcache:
  . Fixed bug #75373 (Warning Internal error: wrong size calculation). (Laruence, Dmitry)

- PGSQL:
  . Fixed bug #75419 (Default link incorrectly cleared/linked by pg_close()). (Sara)

- SOAP:
  . Fixed bug #75464 (Wrong reflection on SoapClient::__setSoapHeaders). (villfa)

- Zlib:
  . Fixed bug #75299 (Wrong reflection on inflate_init and inflate_add). (Fabien
    Villepinte)

26 Oct 2017, PHP 7.1.11

- Core:
  . Fixed bug #75241 (Null pointer dereference in zend_mm_alloc_small()).
    (Laruence)
  . Fixed bug #75236 (infinite loop when printing an error-message). (Andrea)
  . Fixed bug #75252 (Incorrect token formatting on two parse errors in one
    request). (Nikita)
  . Fixed bug #75220 (Segfault when calling is_callable on parent).
    (andrewnester)
  . Fixed bug #75290 (debug info of Closures of internal functions contain
    garbage argument names). (Andrea)

- Apache2Handler:
  . Fixed bug #75311 (error: 'zend_hash_key' has no member named 'arKey' in
    apache2handler). (mcarbonneaux)

- Date:
  . Fixed bug #75055 (Out-Of-Bounds Read in timelib_meridian()). (Derick)

- Hash:
  . Fixed bug #75303 (sha3 hangs on bigendian). (Remi)

- Intl:
  . Fixed bug #75318 (The parameter of UConverter::getAliases() is not
    optional). (cmb)

- litespeed:
  . Fixed bug #75248 (Binary directory doesn't get created when building
    only litespeed SAPI). (petk)
  . Fixed bug #75251 (Missing program prefix and suffix). (petk)

- mcrypt:
  . Fixed bug #72535 (arcfour encryption stream filter crashes php). (Leigh)

- MySQLi:
  . Fixed bug #75018 (Data corruption when reading fields of bit type). (Anatol)

- OCI8:
  . Fixed incorrect reference counting. (Dmitry, Tianfang Yang)

- Opcache
  . Fixed bug #75255 (Request hangs and not finish). (Dmitry)

- PCRE:
  . Fixed bug #75207 (applied upstream patch for CVE-2016-1283). (Anatol)

- PDO_mysql:
  . Fixed bug #75177 (Type 'bit' is fetched as unexpected string). (Anatol)

- SPL:

72

. Fixed bug #73629
(SplDoublyLinkedList::setIteratorMode masks
intern flags).
    (J. Jeising, cmb)

28 Sep 2017, PHP 7.1.10

- Core:
    . Fixed bug #75042 (run-tests.php issues with
EXTENSION block). (John Boehr)

- BCMath:
    . Fixed bug #44995 (bcpowmod() fails if scale !=
0). (cmb)
    . Fixed bug #46781 (BC math handles minus
zero incorrectly). (cmb)
    . Fixed bug #54598 (bcpowmod() may return 1 if
modulus is 1). (okano1220, cmb)
    . Fixed bug #75178 (bcpowmod() misbehaves for
non-integer base or modulus). (cmb)

- CLI server:
    . Fixed bug #70470 (Built-in server truncates
headers spanning over TCP
    packets). (bouk)

- CURL:
    . Fixed bug #75093 (OpenSSL support not
detected). (Remi)

- GD:
    . Fixed bug #75124 (gdImageGrayScale() may
produce colors). (cmb)
    . Fixed bug #75139
(libgd/gd_interpolation.c:1786: suspicious if ?).
(cmb)

- Gettext:
    . Fixed bug #73730 (textdomain(null) throws in
strict mode). (cmb)

- Intl:
    . Fixed bug #75090 (IntlGregorianCalendar
doesn't have constants from parent
    class). (tpunt)
    . Fixed bug #75193 (segfault in
collator_convert_object_to_string). (Remi)

- PDO_OCI:
    . Fixed bug #74631 (PDO_PCO with PHP-FPM:
OCI environment initialized
    before PHP-FPM sets it up). (Ingmar Runge)

- SPL:
    . Fixed bug #75155 (AppendIterator::append() is
broken when appending another
    AppendIterator). (Nikita)
    . Fixed bug #75173 (incorrect behavior of
AppendIterator::append in foreach loop).
    (jhdxr)

- Standard:
    . Fixed bug #75152 (signed integer overflow in
parse_iv). (Laruence)
    . Fixed bug #75097 (gethostname fails if your
host name is 64 chars long). (Andrea)

31 Aug 2017, PHP 7.1.9

- Core:
    . Fixed bug #74947 (Segfault in scanner on INF
number). (Laruence)
    . Fixed bug #74954 (null deref and segfault in

zend_generator_resume()). (Bob)
    . Fixed bug #74725 (html_errors=1 breaks
unhandled exceptions). (Andrea)
    . Fixed bug #75063 (Main CWD initialized with
wrong codepage). (Anatol)
    . Fixed bug #75349 (NAN comparison). (Sara)

- cURL:
    . Fixed bug #74125 (Fixed finding CURL on
systems with multiarch support).
    (cebe)

- Date:
    . Fixed bug #75002 (Null Pointer Dereference in
timelib_time_clone). (Derick)

- Intl:
    . Fixed bug #74993 (Wrong reflection on some
locale_* functions). (Sara)

- Mbstring:
    . Fixed bug #71606 (Segmentation fault
mb_strcut with HTML-ENTITIES encoding).
    (cmb)
    . Fixed bug #62934 (mb_convert_kana() does
not convert iteration marks).
    (Nikita)
    . Fixed bug #75001 (Wrong reflection on
mb_eregi_replace). (Fabien
    Villepinte)

- MySQLi:
    . Fixed bug #74968 (PHP crashes when calling
mysqli_result::fetch_object with
    an abstract class). (Anatol)

- OCI8:
    . Expose oci_unregister_taf_callback() (Tianfang
Yang)

- Opcache:
    . Fixed bug #74980 (Narrowing occurred during
type inference). (Laruence)

- phar:
    . Fixed bug #74991 (include_path has a 4096
char limit in some cases).
    (bwbroersma)

- Reflection:
    . Fixed bug #74949 (null pointer dereference in
_function_string). (Laruence)

- Session:
    . Fixed bug #74892 (Url Rewriting (trans_sid) not
working on urls that start
    with "#"). (Andrew Nester)
    . Fixed bug #74833 (SID constant created with
wrong module number). (Anatol)

- SimpleXML:
    . Fixed bug #74950 (nullpointer deref in
simplexml_element_getDocNamespaces).
    (Laruence)

- SPL:
    . Fixed bug #75049 (spl_autoload_unregister
can't handle
    spl_autoload_functions results). (Laruence)
    . Fixed bug #74669 (Unserialize ArrayIterator
broken). (Andrew Nester)
    . Fixed bug #74977 (Appending AppendIterator
leads to segfault).

(Andrew Nester)
. Fixed bug #75015 (Crash in recursive iterator destructors). (Julien)

- Standard:
. Fixed bug #75075 (unpack with X* causes infinity loop). (Laruence)
. Fixed bug #74103 (heap-use-after-free when unserializing invalid array
    size). (Nikita)
. Fixed bug #75054 (A Denial of Service Vulnerability was found when
    performing deserialization). (Nikita)

- WDDX:
. Fixed bug #73793 (WDDX uses wrong decimal seperator). (cmb)

- XMLRPC:
. Fixed bug #74975 (Incorrect xmlrpc serialization for classes with declared
    properties). (blar)

03 Aug 2017, PHP 7.1.8

- Core:
. Fixed bug #74832 (Loading PHP extension with already registered function
    name leads to a crash). (jpauli)
. Fixed bug #74780 (parse_url() broken when query string contains colon).
    (jhdxr)
. Fixed bug #74761 (Unary operator expected error on some systems). (petk)
. Fixed bug #73900 (Use After Free in unserialize() SplFixedArray). (nikic)
. Fixed bug #74923 (Crash when crawling through network share). (Anatol)
. Fixed bug #74913 (fixed incorrect poll.h include). (petk)
. Fixed bug #74906 (fixed incorrect errno.h include). (petk)

- Date:
. Fixed bug #74852 (property_exists returns true on unknown DateInterval
    property). (jhdxr)

- OCI8:
. Fixed bug #74625 (Integer overflow in oci_bind_array_by_name). (Ingmar Runge)

- Opcache:
. Fixed bug #74623 (Infinite loop in type inference when using HTMLPurifier).
    (nikic)

- OpenSSL:
. Fixed bug #74798 (pkcs7_en/decrypt does not work if \x0a is used in content).
    (Anatol)
. Added OPENSSL_DONT_ZERO_PAD_KEY constant to prevent key padding and fix bug
    #71917 (openssl_open() returns junk on envelope < 16 bytes) and bug #72362
    (OpenSSL Blowfish encryption is incorrect for short keys). (Jakub Zelenka)

- PDO:
. Fixed bug #69356 (PDOStatement::debugDumpParams() truncates query). (Adam
    Baratz)

- SPL:
. Fixed bug #73471 (PHP freezes with AppendIterator). (jhdxr)

- SQLite3:
. Fixed bug #74883 (SQLite3::__construct() produces "out of memory" exception
    with invalid flags). (Anatol)

- Wddx:
. Fixed bug #73173 (huge memleak when wddx_unserialize).
    (tloi at fortinet dot com)

- zlib:
. Fixed bug #73944 (dictionary option of inflate_init() does not work).
    (wapmorgan)

06 Jul 2017, PHP 7.1.7

- Core:
. Fixed bug #74738 (Multiple [PATH=] and [HOST=] sections not properly
    parsed). (Manuel Mausz)
. Fixed bug #74658 (Undefined constants in array properties result in broken
    properties). (Laruence)
. Fixed misparsing of abstract unix domain socket names. (Sara)
. Fixed bug #74603 (PHP INI Parsing Stack Buffer Overflow Vulnerability).
    (Stas)
. Fixed bug #74101, bug #74614 (Unserialize Heap Use-After-Free (READ: 1) in
    zval_get_type). (Nikita)
. Fixed bug #74111 (Heap buffer overread (READ: 1) finish_nested_data from
    unserialize). (Nikita)
. Fixed bug #74819 (wddx_deserialize() heap out-of-bound read via
    php_parse_date()). (Derick)

- Date:
. Fixed bug #74639 (implement clone for DatePeriod and DateInterval).
    (andrewnester)

- DOM:
. Fixed bug #69373 (References to deleted XPath query results). (ttoohey)

- GD:
. Fixed bug #74435 (Buffer over-read into uninitialized memory). (cmb)

- Intl:
. Fixed bug #73473 (Stack Buffer Overflow in msgfmt_parse_message). (libnex)
. Fixed bug #74705 (Wrong reflection on Collator::getSortKey and
    collator_get_sort_key). (Tyson Andre, Remi)

- Mbstring:
. Add oniguruma upstream fix (CVE-2017-9224, CVE-2017-9226, CVE-2017-9227,
    CVE-2017-9228, CVE-2017-9229) (Remi, Mamoru TASAKA)

- OCI8:
. Add TAF callback (PR #2459). (KoenigsKind)

- Opcache:
  . Fixed bug #74663 (Segfault with opcache.memory_protect and validate_timestamp). (Laruence)
  . Revert opcache.enable_cli to default disabled. (Nikita)

- OpenSSL:
  . Fixed bug #74720 (pkcs7_en/decrypt does not work if \x1a is used in content). (Anatol)
  . Fixed bug #74651 (negative-size-param (-1) in memcpy in zif_openssl_seal()). (Stas)

- PDO_OCI:
  . Support Instant Client 12.2 in --with-pdo-oci configure option. (Tianfang Yang)

- Reflection:
  . Fixed bug #74673 (Segfault when cast Reflection object to string with undefined constant). (Laruence)

- SPL:
  . Fixed bug #74478 (null coalescing operator failing with SplFixedArray). (jhdxr)

- FTP:
  . Fixed bug #74598 (ftp:// wrapper ignores context arg). (Sara)

- PHAR:
  . Fixed bug #74386 (Phar::__construct reflection incorrect). (villfa)

- SOAP
  . Fixed bug #74679 (Incorrect conversion array with WSDL_CACHE_MEMORY). (Dmitry)

- Streams:
  . Fixed bug #74556 (stream_socket_get_name() returns '\0'). (Sara)

8 Jun 2017, PHP 7.1.6

- Core:
  . Fixed bug #74600 (crash (SIGSEGV) in _zend_hash_add_or_update_i). (Laruence)
  . Fixed bug #74546 (SIGILL in ZEND_FETCH_CLASS_CONSTANT_SPEC_CONST_CONST). (Laruence)
  . Fixed bug #74589 (__DIR__ wrong for unicode character). (Anatol)

- intl:
  . Fixed bug #74468 (wrong reflection on Collator::sortWithSortKeys). (villfa)

- MySQLi:
  . Fixed bug #74547 (mysqli::change_user() doesn't accept null as $database argument w/strict_types). (Anatol)

- Opcache:
  . Fixed bug #74596 (SIGSEGV with opcache.revalidate_path enabled). (Laruence)

- phar:
  . Fixed bug #51918 (Phar::webPhar() does not handle requests sent through PUT and DELETE method). (Christian Weiske)

- Readline:
  . Fixed bug #74490 (readline() moves the cursor to the beginning of the line). (Anatol)

- Standard:
  . Fixed bug #74510 (win32/sendmail.c anchors CC header but not BCC). (Damian Wadley, Anatol)

- xmlreader:
  . Fixed bug #74457 (Wrong reflection on XMLReader::expand). (villfa)

11 May 2017, PHP 7.1.5

- Core:
  . Fixed bug #74408 (Endless loop bypassing execution time limit). (Laruence)
  . Fixed bug #74353 (Segfault when killing within bash script trap code). (Laruence)
  . Fixed bug #74340 (Magic function __get has different behavior in php 7.1.x). (Nikita)
  . Fixed bug #74188 (Null coalescing operator fails for undeclared static class properties). (tpunt)
  . Fixed bug #74444 (multiple catch freezes in some cases). (David Matějka)
  . Fixed bug #74410 (stream_select() is broken on Windows Nanoserver). (Matt Ficken)
  . Fixed bug #74337 (php-cgi.exe crash on facebook callback). (Anton Serbulov)
  . Patch for bug #74216 was reverted. (Anatol)

- Date:
  . Fixed bug #74404 (Wrong reflection on DateTimeZone::getTransitions). (krakjoe)
  . Fixed bug #74080 (add constant for RFC7231 format datetime). (duncan3dc)

- DOM:
  . Fixed bug #74416 (Wrong reflection on DOMNode::cloneNode). (Remi, Fabien Villepinte)

- Fileinfo:
  . Fixed bug #74379 (syntax error compile error in libmagic/apprentice.c). (Laruence)

- GD:
  . Fixed bug #74343 (compile fails on solaris 11 with system gd2 library). (krakjoe)

- MySQLi:
  . Fixed bug #74432 (mysqli_connect adding ":3306" to $host if $port parameter not given). (Anatol)

- MySQLnd:
  . Fixed bug #74376 (Invalid free of persistent results on error/connection

loss). (Yussuf Khalil)

- Intl:
. Fixed bug #65683 (Intl does not support
DateTimeImmutable). (Ben Scholzen)
. Fixed bug #74298 (IntlDateFormatter-
>format() doesn't return
   microseconds/fractions). (Andrew Nester)
. Fixed bug #74433 (wrong reflection for
Normalizer methods). (villfa)
. Fixed bug #74439 (wrong reflection for Locale
methods). (villfa)

- Opcache:
. Fixed bug #74456 (Segmentation error while
running a script in CLI mode).
   (Laruence)
. Fixed bug #74431 (foreach infinite loop).
(Nikita)
. Fixed bug #74442 (Opcached version produces
a nested array). (Nikita)

- OpenSSL:
. Fixed bug #73833 (null character not allowed in
openssl_pkey_get_private).
   (Jakub Zelenka)
. Fixed bug #73711 (Segfault in
openssl_pkey_new when generating DSA or DH
key). (Jakub Zelenka)
. Fixed bug #74341 (openssl_x509_parse fails to
parse ASN.1 UTCTime without
   seconds). (Moritz Fain)
. Fixed bug #73808 (iv length warning too
restrictive for aes-128-ccm).
   (Jakub Zelenka)

- Readline:
. Fixed bug #74489 (readline() immediately
returns false in interactive
   console mode). (Anatol)

- Standard:
. Fixed bug #72071 (setcookie allows max-age to
be negative). (Craig Duncan)
. Fixed bug #74361 (Compaction in array_rand()
violates COW). (Nikita)

- Streams:
. Fixed bug #74429 (Remote socket URI with
unique persistence identifier
   broken). (Sara)

13 Apr 2017, PHP 7.1.4

- Core:
. Fixed bug #74149 (static embed SAPI linkage
error). (krakjoe)
. Fixed bug #73370 (falsely exits with "Out of
Memory" when using
   USE_ZEND_ALLOC=0). (Nikita)
. Fixed bug #73960 (Leak with instance method
calling static method with
   referenced return). (Nikita)
. Fixed bug #69676 (Resolution of self::FOO in
class constants not correct).
   (Nikita)
. Fixed bug #74265 (Build problems after 7.0.17
release: undefined reference
   to `isfinite'). (Nikita)
. Fixed bug #74302 (yield fromLABEL is over-
greedy). (Sara)

- Apache:
. Reverted patch for bug #61471, fixes bug
#74318. (Anatol)

- Date:
. Fixed bug #72096 (Swatch time value incorrect
for dates before 1970). (mcq8)

- DOM:
. Fixed bug #74004 (LIBXML_NOWARNING flag
ingnored on loadHTML*).
   (somedaysummer)

- iconv:
. Fixed bug #74230 (iconv fails to fail on
surrogates). (Anatol)

- OCI8:
. Fixed uninitialized data causing random crash.
(Dmitry)

- Opcache:
. Fixed bug #74250 (OPcache compilation
performance regression in PHP 5.6/7
   with huge classes). (Nikita)

- OpenSSL:
. Fixed bug #72333 (fwrite() on non-blocking
SSL sockets doesn't work).
   (Jakub Zelenka)

- PDO MySQL:
. Fixed bug #71003 (Expose
MYSQLI_CLIENT_SSL_DONT_VERIFY_SERVER_CE
RT to PDO
   interface). (Thomas Orozco)

- SPL:
. Fixed bug #74058 (ArrayObject can not notice
changes). (Andrew Nester)

- Sqlite:
. Implemented FR #74217 (Allow creation of
deterministic sqlite functions).
   (Andrew Nester)

- Streams:
. Fixed bug #74216 (Correctly fail on invalid IP
address ports). (Sara)

- Zlib:
. Fixed bug #74240 (deflate_add can allocate too
much memory). (Matt Bonneau)

16 Mar 2017, PHP 7.1.3

- Core:
. Fixed bug #74157 (Segfault with nested
generators). (Laruence)
. Fixed bug #74164 (PHP hangs when an invalid
value is dynamically passed to
   typehinted by-ref arg). (Laruence)
. Fixed bug #74093 (Maximum execution time of
n+2 seconds exceed not written
   in error_log). (Laruence)
. Fixed bug #74084 (Out of bound read -
zend_mm_alloc_small). (Laruence).

...

CHAPTER 5

PHP 7.2

This chapter will outline new updates in version 7.2 which is more focused on third party libraries included in the standard PHP package; it also contains new OO improvements.

5.1. New Functionality

5.1.1. Object typing

It is finally possible to use general object notation for specifying a type of the function parameters and the function return output. A generic object will map any custom or built-in classes instances, however it will not resolve correctly to scalar types like: string, int, it also will not match an array.

```
function returnObject(object $obj) : object
{
    return new CustomOrBuildInClass();
}
```

5.1.2. Extending abstract class

So previously PHP 5.x was quite behind with "luxury" object oriented features like constants overloading or extending abstract class. These used to throw a Fatal Exception. Even though extending the abstract class alone was allowed, the method "overriding" was unavailable.

```
abstract class A
{
    abstract function test(string $s);
}
abstract class B extends A
{
    // overridden - still maintaining contravariance for parameters and covariance for return
    abstract function test($s) : int;
}
```

This allows us to copy some of the missing Design Patterns (before unavailable in PHP, but now introduced), and make them more standardised by moving our approach between different languages and ecosystems.

5.1.3. Extension loaded by name

There is now no need to specify any file extension for modules like .dll or .so, as from now on we can enable a PHP setting in *php.ini* file. This also includes an usage of the built-in: dl() function.

```
//php.ini

//all of these will be now acceptable
extension=bz2
extension=php_bz2.dll
extension=bz2.so
extension=bz2.sl
```

5.1.4. Core extension - Sodium

Sodium has become a built-in PHP extension which does not require separate adding or downloading anymore. It is an external, modern and easy to use software library used for encryption, decryption, password hashing and signatures. It's mainly famous for its authentication mechanism, where every piece of encrypted data automatically moves a

Message Authentication Code (MAC), which can validate the integrity of the data itself. When the MAC is invalid, the library will immediately throw an error without any user input.

5.1.5. Extended support for LDAP

LDAP is getting some additional attention from PHP team; it now supports EXOP extension by introducing the following functions and constants:

- `ldap_parse_exop()`

- `ldap_exop()`

- `ldap_exop_passwd()`

- `ldap_exop_whoami()`

- `LDAP_EXOP_START_TLS`

- `LDAP_EXOP_MODIFY_PASSWD`

- `LDAP_EXOP_REFRESH`

- `LDAP_EXOP_WHO_AM_I`

- `LDAP_EXOP_TURN`

5.1.6. Passwords with Argon2

Argon2 has been introduced as a new algorithm available to use for `password_hash()` usages with the following constants:

```
password_hash('abc', PASSWORD_ARGON2I);
password_hash('abc', PASSWORD_ARGON2_DEFAULT_MEMORY_COST);
password_hash('abc', PASSWORD_ARGON2_DEFAULT_TIME_COST);
password_hash('abc', PASSWORD_ARGON2_DEFAULT_THREADS);
```

5.1.7. Parameter type widening

The function arguments are no longer needed to repeat if the implemented method is already defined in the implemented interface. This approach still works with LSP (Liskov Substitution Principle), since the parameters types are contravariant.

```
interface A
{
    public function Test(array $input);
}

class B implements A
{
    public function Test($input){} // no need to repeat the type of array in there
}
```

5.1.8. Grouped namespaces

A trailing comma can be used to specify multiple "use" statements in order to join and chain them into a single call.

```
use Package\Subpackage\{
    First,
    Second,
    Third,
};
//the above will load:
Package\Subpackage\First
Package\Subpackage\Second
Package\Subpackage\Third
```

5.1.9. Unicode support for PDO

For emulating prepares with unicode character strings, PDO has introduced the following constants:

- PDO::PARAM_STR_NATL

- PDO::PARAM_STR_CHAR

- PDO::ATTR_DEFAULT_STR_PARAM

```
$db->quote('über', PDO::PARAM_STR | PDO::PARAM_STR_NATL); // N'über'
$db->quote('A'); // 'A'

$db->setAttribute(PDO::ATTR_DEFAULT_STR_PARAM, PDO::PARAM_STR_NATL);
$db->quote('über'); // N'über'
$db->quote('A', PDO::PARAM_STR | PDO::PARAM_STR_CHAR); // 'A'
```

5.1.10. Debugging information for PDO

The method: `PDOStatement::debugDumpParams()` will now be included with the SQL being sent to the DB, where the full, raw query (including the replaced placeholders with their bounded values) will be shown. The main reason for this feature was to help debugging emulated prepares, which requires enabling the same setting, which is: emulated prepares.

```
//binding PHP variables
$calories = 70;
$colour = 'blue';

$sth = $dbh->prepare('SELECT name, colour, calories
    FROM fruit
    WHERE calories < ? AND colour = ?');
$sth->bindParam(1, $calories, PDO::PARAM_INT);
$sth->bindValue(2, $colour, PDO::PARAM_STR);
$sth->execute();

$sth->debugDumpParams();

//will output:
 SQL: [82] SELECT name, colour, calories
    FROM fruits
    WHERE calories < ? AND colour = ?
Sent SQL: [88] SELECT name, colour, calories
    FROM fruits
    WHERE calories < 70 AND colour = 'blue'
Params:  2
Key: Position #0:
paramno=0
name=[0] ""
```

```
is_param=1
param_type=1
Key: Position #1:
paramno=1
name=[0] ""
is_param=1
param_type=2
```

5.1.11. Additional Sockets support

The Sockets extension has received 4 new functions, which contain outputting of the resources, binding or connecting to a given resource rather than going through the process of creating the socket and connecting themselves. The last function is be responsible for converting the resource to an array for verification.

- `socket_addrinfo_lookup(string node[, mixed service, array hints]) : array`

- `socket_addrinfo_connect(resource $addrinfo) : resource`

- `socket_addrinfo_bind(resource $addrinfo) : resource`

- `socket_addrinfo_explain(resource $addrinfo) : array`

A sample code below would connect and explain the socket information.

```
$info = socket_addrinfo_lookup('localhost', 2000, array('ai_family' => AF_INET,
'ai_socktype' => SOCK_STREAM));
$sockaddr = reset($info);

if (!$sockaddr) {
    die ("Invalid Socket Type");
}
$sock = socket_addrinfo_bind($sockaddr);
// ^^ $sock is a socket resource that is bound to 127.0.0.1:2000 using TCP/IP ready
for reading

//or for just connecting we might use
//$sock = socket_addrinfo_connect($sockaddr);

var_dump(socket_addrinfo_explain($sockaddr));
```

```
//possible output:
array(5) {
  ["ai_flags"]=>
  int(0)
  ["ai_family"]=>
  int(2)
  ["ai_socktype"]=>
  int(1)
  ["ai_protocol"]=>
  int(6)
  ["ai_addr"]=>
  array(2) {
    ["sin_port"]=>
    int(2000)
    ["sin_addr"]=>
    string(9) "127.0.0.1"
  }
}
```

5.1.12. Bytes conversion

The `pack()` and `unpack()` are now being enhanced with additional support of doubles and floats values for 2 rare cases of bytes ordering: Little Endian (where the low-order byte is placed as first, commonly found in: processors x86, DEC VAX) and Big Endian (where the high-order byte is placed as first, used in 32 bits processors).

5.1.13. proc_nice()

This isn't a new function, but it has become available to be used in any Windows hosted environment. The function is changing the priority of the current process on a machine.

5.1.14. PCRE regular expression

PCRE, just like any regular expression package, has now an option to use "J" for PCRE_DUPNAMES, which allows names duplication in subpatterns.

5.1.15. Encrypted ZIPs

You can now encrypt or decrypt your ZIP files by providing additional context of password passed to the `zip://` stream. The `ZipArchive` is now implementing a `Countable` interface to make it compatible with each other.

```
$zip = new ZipArchive();
$res = $zip->open('test.zip', ZipArchive::CREATE);
if ($res === TRUE) {
    $zip->addFromString('test.txt', 'file content goes here');
    $zip->setEncryptionName('test.txt', ZipArchive::EM_AES_256, 'password');
    $zip->close();
    echo 'ok';
} else {
    echo 'failed';
}
```

5.1.16. New bits in EXIF

The EXIF, so the headers from an image file, is now updated to support new data formats. Specific tags are now successfully handled when parsing images with `exif_read_data()`. On top of that, `exif_read_data()` and `exif_thumbnail()` are now expecting streams as their first argument. New supported formats are:

- Samsung

- DJI

- Panasonic

- Sony

- Pentax

- Minolta

- Sigma/Foveon

- AGFA

- Kyocera

- Ricoh

- Epson

5.1.17. SQLite BLOB

The new function has been added to the SQLite3 package called: `openBlob()`, which allows to open BLOB fields in a write mode.

```
public resource SQLite3::openBlob ( string $table , string $column , int $rowid [,
string $dbname = "main" [, int $flags = SQLITE3_OPEN_READONLY ]] )
```

Usage:

```
$conn = new SQLite3(':memory:');
$conn->exec('CREATE TABLE test (text text)');
$conn->exec("INSERT INTO test VALUES ('Lorem ipsum')");
$stream = $conn->openBlob('test', 'text', 1);
echo stream_get_contents($stream);
fclose($stream); // required, otherwise the next line would fail
$conn->close();
```

5.1.18. Oracle failover callbacks

Transparent Application Failover (TAF) callbacks are now available in PHP 7.2. This feature allows OCI8 applications to reconnect automatically to the previously configured database when something with connection goes wrong. This mainly helps in monitoring and controlling the reconnection during failovers.

```
function tafCallback($conn, $event, $type) {
    static $retry_count = 0;
    echo 'event name: '.$event.PHP_EOL;
    echo 'event type: '.$type;

    // Stop retrying after 20 times.
    if (self::$retry_count >= 20) {
        return 0;
    }
    printf(" Failover error received. Trying to sleep for 5 secs...");
    sleep(5);
```

```
        self::$retry_count++;


    if ($event === OCI_FO_END) {
        //service is up again
        echo 'DB is back online';
        return;
    } else {
        //inform about retrying failover
        echo 'retrying..';
        return OCI_FO_RETRY;
    }
}

$connection = oci_connect('hr', 'welcome', 'localhost/XE');
$fn_name = 'tafCallback';

oci_register_taf_callback($connection, $fn_name);

//might return
event name: OCI_FO_ERROR
event type: OCI_FO_SELECT

Failover error received. Trying to sleep for 5 secs...
retrying...

event name: OCI_FO_END
event type: OCI_FO_SELECT

Failover error received. Trying to sleep for 5 secs...
DB is back online
```

Together with register callback function we also have the `oci_unregister_taf_callback()` for resetting the callback.

5.1.19. stream_isatty()

Verifies if a given stream from argument is a valid terminal type device of TTY. Similar function can be already found in PHP previous versions, however `stream_isatty()` can be run on any server; this includes Windows and Linux.

```
php -r "var_export(stream_isatty(STDERR));"
//will return true
```

5.1.20. sapi_window_vt100_support()

The function gets and sets VT100 support for the given stream associated to Windows console output buffer. It takes the first argument as stream and then a flag for enabled or disabled boolean. VT100 might not be available on versions older than Windows 10.

```
php -r "var_export(sapi_windows_vt100_support(STDOUT));echo '
';var_export(sapi_windows_vt100_support(STDERR));" 2>NUL
//will return:
//true false
//as redirect stream does not enable VT100 feature
```

5.1.21. spl_object_id()

Returns an unique identifier for the specified object; the id is only unique until the object is destroyed. Then the same id might be reused for other objects. A similar effect, but with returned hash id, can be achieved by `spl_object_hash()`.

```
$id1 = spl_object_id(new stdClass());
echo $id1.PHP_EOL;

$id2 = spl_object_id(new stdClass());
echo $id2;
//will return
1
2
```

5.1.22. *->count()

A number of classes have introduced a new `count()` method for getting items in the list; these classes are: `DOMNodeList`, `DOMNamedNodeMap` and

`ZIPArchive`. They all implement the `Countable` interface and return `FALSE` if a failure occurs.

5.1.23. ftp_append()

A new FTP function responsible for appending content of a file to the other file on the server.

```
$ftp = ftp_connect('127.0.0.1', $port);
if (!$ftp) die("Couldn't connect to the server");

var_dump(ftp_login($ftp, 'user', 'pass'));
file_put_contents(__DIR__ . '/ftp_append_foo', 'foo');

var_dump(ftp_append($ftp, 'ftp_append_foo', 'ftp_append_foo', FTP_BINARY));
//will return
true
true
```

5.1.24. GD image functions

A number of GD related functions have been added for manipulating clipping images, editing image resolution, bmp conversions and drawing a polygon.

- `imagesetclip()` - sets the rectangle area for clipping;

- `imagegetclip()` - gets the clipping area;

- `imageopenpolygon()` - creates an open polygon off the given image;

- `imageresolution()` - gets or sets the image resolution;

- `imagecreatefrombmp()` - creates an image from BMP source;

- `imagebmp()` - generates a BMP image file.

5.1.25. hash_hmac_algos()

If you ever wanted to figure out which hashing algorithms you can use on your current PHP version, you can now use the `hash_hmac_algos()`, which will give you a list of these algorithms in one go, suitable for `hash_hmac()`.

```
print_r(hash_hmac_algos());
//will return
Array
(
    [0] => md2
    [1] => md4
    [2] => md5
    [3] => sha1
    [4] => sha224
    [5] => sha256
    [6] => sha384
    [7] => sha512/224
...
```

5.1.26. Multibyte Strings

Multi-byte string functions are used mainly to convert strings into different encoding. The MB scheme allows to express more than a standard 256 characters in the regular byte wise coding system. Three new functions have been added to this lot:

- `mb_scrub()` - replace ill-formed byte sequence with substitute characters, for instance: "?";

- `mb_ord()` - gets the character from unicode code point;

- `mb_chr()` - gets the original specific character.

5.2. Fixed bugs

#76677. Enabled opcache no longer causes `call_user_func_array()` used in our example for `strlenb()` (the custom function for returning length of bytes), to return empty value when run from within a context of other function.

```
$token = 'HOME';
$lengthBytes = strlenb($token);
echo "$token $lengthBytes ".($lengthBytes!=0 ? "ok" : "error")."<br>\n";
testString();

function testString()
{
    $token = 'HOME';
    $lengthBytes = strlenb($token);
    echo "$token $lengthBytes ".($lengthBytes!=0 ? "ok" : "error")."<br>\n";
}

function strlenb() { return call_user_func_array("strlen", func_get_args()); }

//before PHP 7.2 it will output:
HOME 3 ok
HOME error
```

#76505. Duplicated subarray keys are now not duplicated when called `array_merge_recursive()` for merging 2 arrays. It used to re-use the same key from the first array for any new first key from the second array. Take a look at the example:

```
$array1 = array(
    'subarray' => array(
        2 => 'first',
        98 => 'second',
    )
);
$array2 = array(
    'subarray' => array(
        6 => 'third'
    )
);

$array3 = array_merge_recursive( $array1, $array2 );
print_r( $array3 );

//pre PHP 7.2.6
Array
```

```
(
    [subarray] => Array
        (
            [2] => first
            [98] => second
            [2] => third
        )
)

//current
Array
(
    [subarray] => Array
        (
            [2] => first
            [98] => second
            [6] => third
        )
)
```

#76502. Previously chained serialized and deserialized data used to not keep the information about Error message when exception was thrown and vice-versa. Therefore it was silently dying without the information stored in `get_class()` output.

```php
$examples = [
    "Error(Exception())"    => new Error("outer", 0, new Exception("inner")),
    "Exception(Error())"    => new Exception("outer", 0, new Error("inner"))
];

foreach ($examples as $name => $example) {
    $processed = unserialize(serialize($example));
    $processedPrev = $processed->getPrevious();
    echo "---- $name ----\n";
    echo "before: ", get_class($example), ".previous == ", get_class($example->getPrevious()), "\n";
    echo "after : ", get_class($processed), ".previous == ", $processedPrev ? get_class($processedPrev) : "null", "\n";
}

//pre PHP 7.2
---- Error(Exception()) ----
```

```
before: Error.previous == Exception
after : Error.previous == null
---- Exception(Error()) ----
before: Exception.previous == Error
after : Exception.previous == null

//current
---- Error(Exception()) ----
before: Error.previous == Exception
after : Error.previous == Error
---- Exception(Error()) ----
before: Exception.previous == Error
after : Exception.previous == Exception
```

#76459. Security restriction is now available for `linkinfo()` on Windows environments. Previously we could go beyond the `open_basedir` location, which is quite insecure, as potential attack could scan our whole file directory.

```
$var1="c:\\jump";
print "checking $var1 ...".PHP_EOL;
print @linkinfo($var1).PHP_EOL;
$var1="c:\\jump\\folder\\file1.txt";
print "checking $var1 ...".PHP_EOL;
print @linkinfo($var1).PHP_EOL;
$var1="c:\\jump\\blabla";
print "checking $var1 ...".PHP_EOL;
print @linkinfo($var1).PHP_EOL;

//pre PHP 7.2.6
C:\php726\php.exe -n -dopen_basedir=C:\tools sample.php
checking c:\jump ...
2
checking c:\jump\folder\file1.txt ...
2
checking c:\jump\blabla ...
-1

//current
Warning: linkinfo(): open_basedir restriction in effect...
```

#76333. Internal PHP server can now find files and run if the root directory contains special characters in the file path.

```
C:\weirdĄŚfolder\
echo "sample contents" > test.txt
php -S localhost:8000

//pre PHP 7.2.5
[Sat May 12 14:07:18 2018] ::1:50023 [404]: /test.txt - No such file or directory

//current
[Sat May 12 14:06:33 2018] ::1:50018 [200]: /test.txt
```

#76287. In some cases where the modulus was provided as a negative number, modulus arbitrary precision number is now returning correct results for `bcmod()` function.

```
$leftOperand = '0.00000000099999';
$modulus = '-0.00056';
$scale =14;

echo bcmod($leftOperand,$modulus, $scale);

//pre PHP 7.2.5
0.00000000099999

//current
-0.00055999900001
```

#75597. Large strings (larger than 16K) passed in `CURLOPT_POSTFIELDS` are now correctly passed to the server and not truncated and cut into repeated blocks.

```
$string = array(0 => "ABCDEFGHIJKLMN.."); // make sure you have more than
20000 length
..
curl_setopt($s, CURLOPT_POST, true);
curl_setopt($s, CURLOPT_POSTFIELDS, $string );
...
```

```
//pre PHP 7.2 (notice repetitions)
"ABCDEFABCDEFABCD.."
```

```
//current
"ABCDEFGHIJKLMN..."
```

#74953. Default locale is now used when passing a `NULL` value as the second argument to the `Locale::getDisplayName()` method.

```
//both of the above will match if getDefault() will return English locale
Locale::getDisplayName('sl-Latn-IT-nedis', 'en');
Locale::getDisplayName('sl-Latn-IT-nedis');
```

#74974. Comparing to `NaN` (Not a Number), it is now fixed in the newest PHP version. Unexpected results are mainly reported when `NaN` is combined against lower/higher than operators.

```
$nan = NAN;

if (0 < NAN) { echo 'TRUE'; } else { echo 'FALSE'; }
echo "\n";
if (0 < $nan) { echo 'TRUE'; } else { echo 'FALSE'; }

//pre PHP 7.2
TRUE
FALSE

//current
TRUE
TRUE
```

#74941. `session_start()` no longer displays a warning message when there aren't any headers output by itself, but some other pieces of code already returned some headers.

```
ini_set('session.use_cookies', false);
ini_set('session.cache_limiter', false);

echo 'some text';
```

```
session_start();

//pre PHP 7.2
Warning: session_start(): Cannot start session when headers already sent in
test.php on line 8

Call Stack:
    0.0001    397720    1. {main}() test.php:0
    0.0001    398128    2. session_start() test.php:8

//current
No warning triggered.
```

5.3. Deprecated elements

5.3.1. Unquoted strings

Unquoted strings now return E_WARNING.

5.3.2. png2wbmp() and jpeg2wbmp()

Both PNG functions have been retired and are replaced with
imagecreatefrompng() and imagewbmp().

5.3.3. __autoload() method

Magic function of __autoload() is no longer the preferred way of
attaching loading logic. Now you need to use
spl_autoload_register(), which gives an ability to register multiple
autoloaders instead of just 1.

5.3.4. track_errors ini setting and $php_errormsg variable

The preferred way of retrieving the error information is by using
error_get_last().

5.3.5. create_function()

Too many security issues have caused this function to be left without support. The preferred alternative is to use anonymous functions.

5.3.6. parse_str() without a second argument

This function should always be used with two arguments, as the second argument causes the query string to be parsed into an array.

5.3.7. Function gmp_random()

When you generate a random number by the GMP extension, use `gmp_random_bits()` and `gmp_random_range()` instead.

5.3.8. Function each()

This function is slower than foreach, but works in the same manner.

5.3.9. Function assert() with a string argument

Using `assert()` with a string argument may cause a remote code execution hack, so it won't be supported.

5.3.10. Function read_exif_data()

The `exif_read_data()` function should be used instead.

CHAPTER 6.
PHP 7.3

In this chapter we will look at some of the great new features of PHP 7.3.

6.1. New Functionality

6.1.1. Flexible Heredoc and Nowdoc

The heredoc and nowdoc syntaxes have very rigid requirements. This has caused them to be, in-part, eschewed by developers because the usage in code can look ugly and harm the readability. Therefore, this option suggests two changes to the current heredoc and nowdoc syntaxes:

```
//Enabling the closing marker to be indented, and removing the newline requirement
after the closing marker

//PHP 7.2
$html = '<ul>';
$html .= '<li>foo</li>';
$html .= '<li>bar</li>';
$html .= '<li>baz</li>';
$html = '</ul>';

//PHP 7.3
$html = <<<html
<ul>
    <li>foo</li>
    <li>bar</li>
```

```
    <li>baz</li>
  </ul>
  html
```

The only difference between heredoc and nowdoc is that heredoc performs string interpolation, turning your variables into the string they represent, while nowdoc does not.

6.1.2. Trailing commas in function calls

The ability to have a trailing comma in arrays is already built-in, so why not have it extended to function/method parameters? This will easily allow us to pass a dynamic list of arguments created on the fly without many problems. It will also grant the possibility to keep that last comma, like it does for arrays when we list arguments for function per lines, below. Of course leading commas and multiple commas still won't be allowed and will cause the syntax error. You cannot use more than one comma at the end or use commas to skip arguments.

```
//new allowed cases
unset(
    $foo,
    $bar,
    $baz,
);

array_merge(
    $array1,
    $array2,
    ['one', two'],
);

$object->methodName(
  'first',
  'second',
);
```

6.1.3. References in list()

In PHP 7.3 you can now use references in `list()` calls or any other array creations. The syntax is a standard ampersand prefixed variable which will shorthand some of the use cases when using complex array integrations.

```
$arr = [1, 2];
list($a, &$b) = $arr;

//will match the:
$a = $arr[0];
$b =& $arr[1];

//plus it will work as:
[$a, &$b] = $array;
```

6.1.4. First and last array keys

There are new functions added to array package: `array_key_first()` and `array_key_last()` for getting the first or last key of the array. This is extremely useful when the array is not an index based one and we don't know its keys. These functions will not affect the internal array pointer.

```
$array = ['a' => 1, 'b' => 2, 'c' => 3];

echo array_key_first($array);
echo array_key_last($array);

//will return
a
c
```

6.1.5. Unset variables in compact()

This change, even though marked as a feature/enhancements, looks a bit like a bug fix actually. The bottom line was shown when we passed an undefined variable to `compact()`, then, instead of triggering an appropriate E_NOTICE issue, it'd silently skip it. From now on, the warning message is thrown as expected by majority.

```
// the below line will now throw an Undefined variable: invalid_var
$combined = compact('invalid_var');
```

6.2. Fixed bugs

#76700. Fixed error when you try call to a protected method by trait aliases.

```
trait T1
{
    protected function foo() { echo 'bar'; }
}

trait T2
{
    use T1 {
        foo as public;
    }
}

class A
{
    use T1;
}

class B extends A
{
    use T2;
}

$b = new B();
$b->foo();

Output
bar
```

#76610. Fixed fatal error when ",‟ is missing for not last element in array.

```
$headers = array(
    'From' => 'webmaster@example.com',
    'Reply-To' => 'webmaster@example.com'
    'X-Mailer' => 'PHP/' . phpversion()
);
```

#76443. Fixed the usage of `php+php_interbase.dll` in Extensions calls on Winodws 7, which use to produce: `Unhandled exception at 0x7789BA26 (ntdll.dll) in php.exe` error. Sample *.bat* file which was broken before:

```
php phpinfo.php or php-cgi phpinfo.php, where phpinfo.php =
<?php phpinfo();?>

php.ini:
[PHP]
extension_dir = "ext"
extension=interbase
```

#76564. The ZIP extension (ext/zip) now works correctly via Extensions calls ext/zip on Windows 10. The following .bat file will no longer error with the stack trace:

```
@echo off
cscript /nologo configure.js  "--disable-all" "--enable-cli" "--enable-zts" "--enable-zip"
"--enable-debug-pack" %*
```

6.3. Deprecated elements

6.3.1. The declaration and use of case-insensitive constants

The declaration and use of case-insensitive constants has been deprecated.

6.3.2. image2wbmp

Outputs the image to browser or file. `image2wbmp()` is deprecated as of PHP 7.3.0, and will be removed in the next major version.

CHAPTER 7

PHP 7.4

Even though PHP 7.4 has not been officially announced, there is some information stating that 7.4 may never be released. At the time of writing this book, there is still an open debate within the PHP core development team about releasing PHP 8 after 7.3. "It's all up to debate as that's largely based on what the team will decide to scope for version 8".

7.1. New Functionality

As of October 2018, there isn't any official news on a new official feature list included in the next version of PHP. However, we have a list of potential accepted RFCs (Requests for Changes) which are included in the PHP 7.4/8, outlined below and in the Chapter 9. *https://wiki.php.net/rfc#implemented*

7.1.1. Same site cookies

The concept of origin cookies read only by the creator is already known in Chrome and Firefox. PHP frameworks already implement such cookie option in a custom way; this is why PHP is now getting a built-in support of setting any cookie with Same Site flag. This flag can take two forms: Lax - available on any website that tries to toad it and Strict - will only allow a cookie to be read by original website. The above change will be adopted to a number of functions below by introducing it together with new parameter options of array type to pass it over as the second or fourth parameter:

- `setcookie()`

- `setrawcookie()`

- `session_set_cookie_params()`

7.1.2. Typed properties

After not great start in 2011, there is a finally confirmed Class Typed Properties to be introduced in 7.4 version. These properties could be of any available type (apart from `callable` and `void`) and introduce some limitation when using inheritance to prevent from changing the types in child's class. This will include any static properties as well as usage of ? mark to inform that the variable could be also a `NULL` value.

```
class MyTypedClass {
    public int $scalarType;
    protected ClassName $classType;
    private ?ClassName $nullableClassType;

    // available to static
    public static iterable $staticProp;

    // default values
    public string $str = "foo";
    public ?string $nullableStr = null;

    // usage for many vars in single line
    public float $x, $y;
}

//inheritance limitations:
class First {
    private bool $a;
    public int $b;
    public ?int $c;
}
class Second extends First {
```

```
    public string $a; // all fine as First::$a is private
    public ?int $b;   // error
    public int $c;    // error
}
```

There is also a plan to introduce support of multiple types called: Union Types, which would allow to provide a list of combined types for the single var, for instance:

```
class MyClass {
    public int|string $a;
    public array|string $b;
}
```

However this is marked as pending work for future whereas the Typed Properties are something which prototype already exists.

7.2 Fixed bugs

So far the version hasn't been released so there aren't any targeted bugs associated with it.

7.3. Proposed deprecated elements

7.3.1. enable_dl() php.ini directive

The function `enable_dl()` does not make sense since in v5.3 when it was available only via CLI, because any CLI user could easily bypass it anyway. A proposed change is to add a warning message if `enable_dl` is not zero.

7.3.2. The 'real' float type

Currently in PHP a float type can have two aliases: double and real (very rarely used).

Hence it is marked as deprecated for real type-cast when a check of `is_real()` is made.

7.3.3. The hebrev() and hebrevc() functions

Before browsers properly supported the conversion of RTL to LTR (hebrew language), the functions: `hebrev()` and `hebrevc()` were used to address that problem. However, now all modern browsers are already handling that issue properly so there is no need to keep these functions in the scope anymore.

7.3.4. Magic Quotes

The hated magic quotes configurations were removed in PHP 5.4, while the built-in functions were still available to use but they were always returning a FALSE. So it makes sense to deprecate them entirely; this includes both: `get_magic_quotes_gpc()` and `get_magic_quotes↪ _runtime()`.

7.3.5. __CLASS__ constant

Since the version 5.5 we can get a class name out of the class by calling `self::class` or by `ClassName::class`. Hence `__CLASS__` constant is marked as no longer supported.

7.3.6. get_called_class()

Same as in previous example a `get_called_class()` can be easily replaced by `static::class` usage, which gives better and more reliable results.

7.3.7. array_key_exists() with objects

This function behaves similarly to `property_exists()` from the legacy point of view. But it was never a recommended way of checking the objects, so this behaviour should be deprecated too.

7.3.8. FILTER_SANITIZE_MAGIC_QUOTES

Removed magic quotes call within `addslashes()` function can be easily mimic by `add_slashes(FILTER_SANITIZE_ADD_SLASHES)` as it still might be useful for some cases. This is why `FILTER_SANITIZE↪ _MAGIC_QUOTES` will be discouraged as well.

7.3.9. INPUT_SESSION & INPUT_REQUEST

This one is a bit weird, as `INPUT_SESSION` and `INPUT_REQUEST`, so the input types for the filter extensions, were never implemented and simply did not work at all, so no wonder these usages will be prompted with `E_WARNING` message.

7.3.10. apache_request_headers()

The Apache specific function name is available for more than just an Apache. The global handler for these is: `getallheaders()` function which does the same thing but has a better support for other servers. Hence, there is no point in using this function at all.

CHAPTER 8.
PHP 8.0

Even though PHP 8 has not been officially released, there are some more certain features that will be included in next major version and some features less likely to be carried out in version 8.

8.1. New Functionality

8.1.1. Just-In-Time

A current standard way of executing PHP is the process of compiling and then executing the resulted code. This is also called Zend Engine in PHP. The Just-In-Time is a type of dynamic transaction that includes compilation during the execution of a program. This approach can result in a much quicker output and can reduce the waiting time for an end user. Facebook is already using a custom made JIT compilation called HHVM instead of the Zend Engine. JIT will most likely overcome the inefficiency of interpreting Opcode, which is an existing internal code cache.

The new JIT integration implementation started in late 2014, however for unknown reasons this particular extension hasn't been released since then, but is very likely to be included in PHP 8. Even though JIT is a major improvement, it might not give a fast push to the web-based websites due to the nature of these projects. The best cases for Just-In-

Time compilation are all continuously running process, like Java or Node.js. This can lead to creation of sandbox running PHP similar to Node.js approach, but this has not been mentioned anywhere yet.

8.1.2. TypeError

Even though `TypeErrors` have been introduced in 7.0, not all the areas have been updated yet. Some of the sections still fail by returning NULLs. The most userland function already throws them, but the internal function still has some edge cases and wrong behaviours. This particular issues will be address in next major PHP release.

8.1.3. Merge Class Member Symbols

There are some inconsistencies between the case sensitivities and insensitivities between the class constants, properties and methods. This will be changed to insensitivities option to all, in order to unify every available case, which might impact some of the existing classes. However, there are still some limitations when calling dynamic variables or when evaluating dynamic method calls. Here are some examples, which will be fixed:

```php
class MyClass {
    const name = 'constant';
    const anotherVar = 'another const';

    public static $name = 'property';
    public static function name() {
        return 'method #1';
    }

    public function name2() {
        return 'method #2';
    }
}


$name = 'anotherVar';
//can't call dynamically a variable off class if the name is already used inside:
MyClass::$name
```

110

```
//will return: constant
```

```
$name2 = function() { echo 'internal function'; };
$this->$name2()
//will return 'method #2' as it will map the method name first, which is wrong
```

8.1.4. Merge Constant, Function and Class Symbols

Functions like `array_map()` or `usort()`, which use callable objects as arguments, are not recognizing properly any internal PHP functions passed in a normal way, instead they expect strings with function names or arrays with class & method definitions instead. This enhancement allows the use of symbols like classes, interfaces or traits to be called directly.

```
//pre PHP.8, which could cause typos and errors
array_map('strlen', $array);
usort($array, array('MyClass', 'methodName'));
```

```
//PHP 8
array_map(strlen, $array);
usort($array, MyClass::methodName());
```

8.1.5. Improved instanceof and subtype

The existing function `instanceof` will start supporting standard primary types like: `string`, `int`, `float` or `array`. In addition to that there will be two new added functions: `is_type_of()` and `is_subtype_of()`. The subtype check will include a check of the whole type hierarchy, whereas the type check will only compare with the bottom level of type.

```
//enhanced instaneof
if ($int instanceof int)
```

```
//new type check
is_type_of(2, int)
```

```
//new subtype check
is_subtype_check([1, 2], iterable)
```

8.1.6. Class and abstract type errors

The Type Errors are introduced but in the case of extended interfaces or abstract classes, when you trigger the "..must be compatible with.." or "...should be compatible...", then it still throws Fatal Errors instead of the Throwable objects.

```
abstract class A {
    public function test($foo) {


    }
}

abstract class B extends A {
    public function test(string $foo) {


    }
}

interface I {
    public function test($foo);
}

class C implements I {
    public function test(string $foo) {


    }
}

//pre PHP8
Warning: Declaration of B::test(string $foo) should be compatible with A::test($foo)
in /in/hamQi on line 13
Fatal error: Declaration of C::test(string $foo) must be compatible with I::test($foo)
in /in/hamQi on line 19
```

8.1.7. Return true

Some methods and functions in existing public interfaces are always returning TRUE, even though their documentation says they should return VOID or boolean. The list mainly includes the SPL codebase like:

`SplHelp::insert` or `SplDoublyLinkedList::push`, however there are also included functions like: `array_walk()` or `Locale::setDefault`. The full list be will defined and published when this feature is approved into PHP8 scope.

8.1.8. Foreign Function Interface

The Foreign Function Interface (FFI) is a simple way to call any native functions, access variables or create data structures defined in original C language. The solution is in the experimental extension that could be already used in PHP 7.3+; the library is libffi and allows a high level languages to generate C code. The github page is: *https://github.com/↪ dstogov/php-ffi*. An example usage is provided below:

```php
//php code
$libc = new FFI("
    //start of C code
    int printf(const char *format, ...);
    const char * getenv(const char *);
    unsigned int time(unsigned int *);

    typedef unsigned int time_t;
    typedef unsigned int suseconds_t;

    struct timeval {
        time_t     tv_sec;
        suseconds_t tv_usec;
    };

    struct timezone {
        int tz_minuteswest;
        int tz_dsttime;
    };

     int gettimeofday(struct timeval *tv, struct timezone *tz);
     //end of C code
", "libc.so.6");

$libc->printf("Hello World from %s!\n", "PHP");
var_dump($libc->getenv("PATH"));
var_dump($libc->time(null));
```

```
$tv = $libc->new("struct timeval");
$tz = $libc->new("struct timezone");
$libc->gettimeofday(FFI::addr($tv), FFI::addr($tz));
var_dump($tv->tv_sec, $tv->tv_usec, $tz);

//will output
Hello World from PHP!
string(135) "/usr/lib64/qt-
3.3/bin:/usr/lib64/ccache:/usr/local/bin:/usr/bin:/bin:/usr/local/sbin:/usr/sbin:/home/
dmitry/.local/bin:/home/dmitry/bin"
int(1523617815)
int(1523617815)
int(977765)
object(FFI\CData:<struct>)#3 (2) {
  ["tz_minuteswest"]=>
  int(-180)
  ["tz_dsttime"]=>
  int(0)
}
```

8.1.9. Covariant Returns and Parameters

This feature will improve the scalar return and parameter types by extending their list with more broad types like: mixed, object, scalar, iterable or numeric. That will allow providing subtyping from base type in interface (for example) to the top type in the class implementation.

```
//object and class example
interface Factory {
    function make(): object;
}

class UserFactory implements Factory {
    function make(): User;
}

//iterable and array
class Collection implements Concatable {
    // accepts all iterables, not just Traversables
    function concat(iterable $input) {/* . . . */}
}
```

```
class MyCollection implements Collection {
    function concat(array $input) {/* . . . */}
}
```

8.2. Potential new features

8.2.1. Arrays with negative index

The arrays are now getting a proper and responsive negative index support. This means that we can not only specify a negative index as array key, but also if we start populating an array from a negative number, then any other pushed element will follow the pattern: 'index + 1'.

```
$array = [-2: false];
$array[] = true;
$array[] = true;
var_dump($array);

//PHP 7
array(3) {
  [-2]=>
  bool(false)
  [0]=>
  bool(true)
  [1]=>
  bool(true)
}

//PHP 8
array(3) {
  [-2]=>
  bool(false)
  [-1]=>
  bool(true)
  [0]=>
  bool(true)
}
```

8.2.2. APXS LoadModule

A new configuration flag (`-with-apxs2-hook[=TYPE]`) was added. It appends Apache's main configuration file (*httpd.conf*) to the `LoadModule` statement. The advantage of Apache Extension Tool APXS is a number of available options to use by enabling/disabling PHP extension to specify the path to PAX. The script is also responsible for generating the *Makefile*.

8.2.3. DateTime and Daylight Saving Time Transitions

The `DateTime` object already supports the Daylight Saving Time swap, however it will only be taken into account when an user passes a timezone either by timezone offset (f.e. -2000), by timezone code (f.e. PST) or by a `DateTimeZone` object passed as a second argument. If the `DateTime` does not receive a timezone, it still uses the default timezone set by a server or via `date_default_timezone_set()`, but it does not translate the Daylight Saving Time at all in these cases. The feature is to include the timezone check into every example.

There is also going to be added another formatter called: DST or ST, which is used to include or exclude the check for Daylight Saving Time or Standard Time (for backwards compatibilities). The lack of this format is default in DST format.

```
//these 3 cases works fine pre PHP8
$d = new DateTime('2018-09-13 14:15:16 -0400');
$d = new DateTime('2018-09-13 14:15:16 EDT');
$d = new DateTime('2018-09-13 14:15:16', new
DateTimeZone('America/New_York'));

//these ones will work after PHP8
$d = new DateTime('2018-09-13 14:15:16');
$d = new DateTime('2018-09-13 14:15:16 DST');
```

In the STD and swap, the time between 2:00:00 am and 2:59:59 am does not exist during the Forward Transitions transition. Any attempts in create it will be rounded forward, just as PHP does for trying to create a February 29th on a non-leap year.

```
date_default_timezone_set('America/New_York');
```

```
//try to create datetime at non-existing time during the STD
$date = new DateTime('2018-03-14 02:30:00');
echo $date->format('Y-m-d H:i:s T');
;
//will return (notice the hour change)
2018-03-14 03:30:00 EDT
```

8.2.4. E_WARNING for invalid containers

Provides improved support for accessing non array/string variables and
displaying E_WARNING message when situations like that happen. This
again could potential looks like bug fix, but it has a big impact on other
sections of PHP. The first one creates a small delay around accessing the
invalid variable we are trying to get. Previously the array accessed
variable was just returning NULL instead of saying anything went wrong,
which was confusing for developers on its expected behaviour. Affected
sections of this feature are: error_get_last(), list(), is_scalar()
or passing by reference.

```
//pre PHP8
$a = false;
var_dump ($a[5]);
//will return
NULL

//PHP8
$a = false;
var_dump ($a[5]);
//will return
E_WARNING Accessing index of non-array or string object
```

8.3. Deprecated elements

Nothing so far.

CHAPTER 9.

Performance benchmark

Important. This chapter aims to show differences in performance between versions of PHP, not between PHP frameworks.

For each test, we will use the same machine and configuration to eliminate all the variables.

Specification:

CPU - 4vCore @2GHz
RAM- 8 GB
Storage Platform- Ceph
OS - Ubuntu 14.04
Virtualization - Virtuozzo

9.1. WordPress 4.9.8

WordPress is the most popular CMS based on PHP. Wordpress was released on May 27, 2003, by Matt Mullenweg and Mike Little. Of course the tested version is from August 2, 2018.

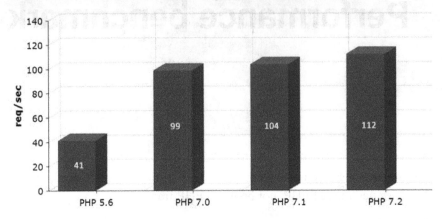

Image 9.1.

9.2. Laravel 5.4

Laravel is a free, open-source PHP web framework. It is currently at the top of the list of the most popular PHP frameworks.

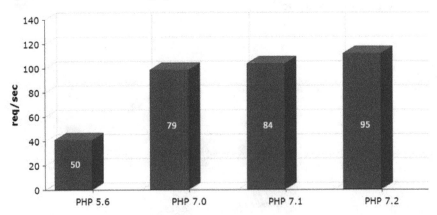

Image 9.2.

9.3. Symfony 3

Symfony is a "big" PHP framework. Some love it, others hate it. In any case, it could not be missed in any benchmark.

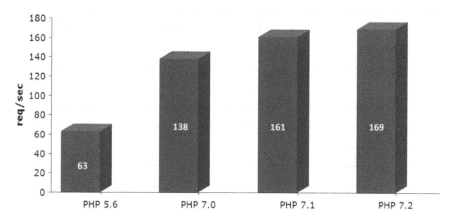

Image 9.3.

9.4. Drupal 8

Drupal is a very popular open-source CMS with strong community.

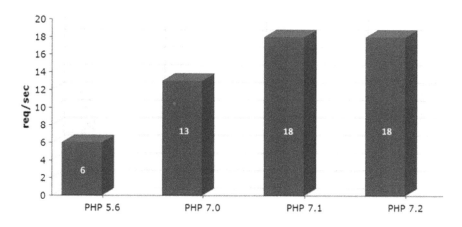

Image 9.4.

9.5. Joomla! 3.8.11

Joomla is another open-source CMS based on PHP MVC pattern.

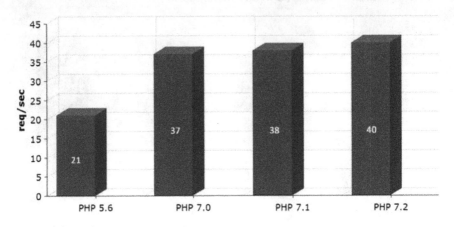

Image 9.5.

9.6. PrestaShop v 1.7.4.2

PrestaShop is currently one of the leading e-commerce systems. Thanks to the huge amount of add-ons, it is a complete tool to use for developer.

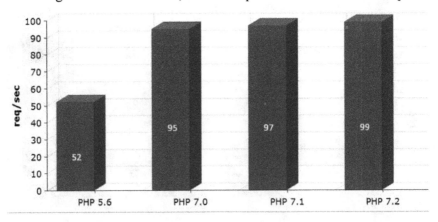

Image 9.6.

9.7. Magento 2.3.0-alpha release

Magento is one of the most popular e-commerce systems written in PHP.

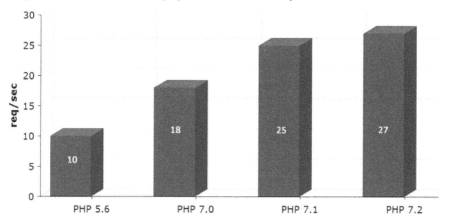

Image 9.7.

CHAPTER 10

Pitfalls

Here are some handful tips to help avoid most common mistakes using new versions of PHP.

10.1. Too frequent use of object type

Example:

```php
<?php
declare(strict_types=1);

class foo
{
    public $spam = 'lorem';
}

class bar
{
    public $eggs = 4;
}

function myFunction(object $bar): string
{
    return sprintf("Output: %d", $bar->eggs);
}

echo myFunction(new foo);
```

```
//output: Notice: Undefined property: foo::$eggs
```

As you can see in the above example, the only information we see is that `myFunction()` expects an object from us. We do not know which specific class is an object that causes quite a stir and errors.

We do not have any specific information on which method is expected. In order to find out what kind of object we need to use, we have to follow the implementation and then deduce it ourselves. Unfortunately, the error that will be returned does not describe the real reason why it was created.

Let's see how a solution with a more specific error could look like:

```php
<?php
declare(strict_types=1);

interface Home {}

interface Office {}

class Room implements Home
{
    public $status = 'clean';
}

class Desk  implements Office
{
    public $width = 200;
}

function deskWidth(Office $desk): string
{
    return sprintf("Desk width : %d centimeters", $desk->width);
}

echo deskWidth(new Room);
//Output: PHP Fatal error:  Uncaught TypeError: Argument 1 passed to deskWidth()
must implement interface Office, instance of Room given.
```

Now the error better informs us what argument the `deskWidth()` function expects. However, this is not over. The object type can also be used for returning.

```php
<?php declare(strict_types=1);
class Home
{
    public $status= 'clean';
}

class Vehicle {}


function getStatus(Home $home): object
{
    return new Vehicle;
}
```

In this situation, only the developer knows that the `getStatus()` function returns an object, but it can be any object. Of course, the object type is not useless. It is always better to have an information that the object is returned than no information at all, but you need to specify the object type as narrowly as you can. If you expect `Home` object do not use "`object`", use "`Home`", instead:

```php
class Home {}
function myFunction(Home $home): Home
{
    return new Home;
}
```

10.2. Method return value

This is the most commonly made mistake by developers who have moved from PHP 5 to 7. Before we were unable to use method return value in write context as it was causing to display a Fatal Error. In order to bypass this situation we were forced to assign the method result to the variable and then perform a check on it. Since PHP 7 (but also in the most recent of 5.5) we do not need to do that any more.

```php
class abc {
    public function getMe() {
        return true;
    }
}
```

```
$object = new abc();

if (empty($object->getMe())) {
    echo 'getMe is empty';
} else {
    echo 'getMe is not empty';
}

//PHP5
Fatal error</b>: Can't use method return value in write context in file.php on line
12

//PHP 7
getMe is not empty
```

10.3. Use of unserialize()

The new filtered `unserialize()` feature introduced in PHP7 does allow now to provide a better security by providing a whitelist classes than can be allowed to unserialize. But even with this, passing unknown input to `unserialize()` can still cause some security holes. Unserialization can result in code being executed due to autoloading and instantiation. A safer way for importing and exporting content out is by using a JSON related functions like `json_encode()` and `json_decode()`.

10.4. Class Autoloading

Providing autloading in opposed to standard `require` or `include` statements is a big performance boost. In first approach you only get a content of separate file when you asked for specific class object. Where as a second option includes every file every single time of the request. In PHP7 we can now provide many different rules around different locations and structure of the external libraries by using `spl_autoload_register()`.

```
//load own classes
function loadMyClasses($class){
    echo 'Loading our custom class: ' . $class;
    include_once('classes/' . $class . '.php');
}

spl_autoload_register('loadMyClasses');

//load 3rd party library classes via anonymous function
spl_autoload_register(function ($class){
    echo 'We are loading 3rd party class: ' . $class;
    include_once('vendor/lib_name/classes/' . $class . '.inc.php');
});
```

10.5. Overload the abstract method

PHP 7.2 allows you to overload the abstract method.

```php
<?php
declare(strict_types=1);

class Bar
{
}

abstract class Foo {
    abstract public function getAnimalSound(string $tone): Bar;
}

class Baz extends Foo
{
    public function getSth($varible): Bar
    {
    }
}
```

In PHP 7.1 we will get Fatal Error but in PHP 7.2 everything works fine. It means that the variable `$varible` does not have to be the string type in this case. This is confusing.

Let's see now what we get with the use of interface:

```
declare(strict_types=1);

interface Foo {
    public function getSth(Bar $variable): string;
}

class Bar {}


class Baz implements Foo
{
    public function getSth($varible): string
    {
    }
}
```

Unlike the previous code, this one no longer generates any errors, which means that the `$varible` variable can be any type, not just `Bar`. The new rules may be a bit confusing, which is why we have to take special care when using them.

CHAPTER 11.
Summary

In the above chapters, we discussed how PHP changed from version 5.6 to the unofficially announced PHP 8. The biggest breakthrough are, as can be observed, versions 5.5 and 7.x. We received not only more tools but also a huge efficiency jump. PHP 7 runs on a brand new PHPNG (PHP Next Generation) engine. This change has enabled us to achieve a 100% increase in speed. Performance improvements can be seen in the Performance Benchmark charts. However, improved performance is not everything. The error handling has also been improved thanks to `EngineException`. 64-bit support for Windows. New operators. Anonymous Classes...

Summing up, version 7 is brutally better than the previous ones on every level. However, we need to remember that older versions of popular systems like Magento do not support PHP version 7. Before we decide to upgrade, we need to make sure our code is compatible with the latest version of PHP. We recommend that you read the Deprecated sections included in every chapter.

And if you are still curious, we invite you to the Appendix section where you will find non-family solutions using PHP :)

More information about bugs, new releases and features of new PHP can be found on: *https://bugs.php.net*, *http://php.net* and *https://wiki.php.net*.

CHAPTER 12.
Appendix

This section will cover various aspects of PHP, which are not that popular but still deserve few words of mention.

12.1. PHP-GTK

Have you ever thought of PHP as a language for more than just a server side scripting solution? Well, you are not the first one; the mystical project of PHP-GTK, available under the address: *http://gtk.php.net/* is another use case of PHP. The PHP-GTK is a tool for writing native, desktop applications written completely in PHP! Yes, you are hearing it right, this PHP extension implements language binding and interface of GTK classes and functions. The whole project was established in 2001 by Andrei Zmiveski. The main author's argumentation for it was: "I did it because I wanted to see if it was possible". Unfortunately the project is dead since PHP 5.5 and it doesn't look like it's going to be updated any time soon. A more recent alternative is a PHP Desktop project, which looks like more up to date and is still working. This can be found on: *https://github.com/cztomczak/phpdesktop*. A sample PHP-GTK application for logging in an displaying a right/wrong messages can be inspected below:

```php
<?php
```

```php
/**
 * Here we create a login window.
 * It has a username and a password field, and a
 * Cancel and Login button. Some error checking
 * is being done when the user clicks "Login".
 */

if (!class_exists('gtk')) {
    die("Please load the php-gtk2 module in your php.ini\r\n");
}


/**
 * This function gets called as soon as the user
 * clicks on the Login button.
 *
 * @param GtkWindow $wnd        The login window, needed to close it
 *                              when all is ok
 * @param GtkEntry $txtUsername  The username text field, used to get
 *                              the username
 * @param GtkEntry $txtPassword  The password widget to retrieve the
 *                              password
 */
function login(GtkWindow $wnd, GtkEntry $txtUsername, GtkEntry $txtPassword)
{
    //fetch the values from the widgets into variables
    $strUsername = $txtUsername->get_text();
    $strPassword = $txtPassword->get_text();

    //Do some error checking
    $errors = null;
    if (strlen($strUsername) == 0) {
        $errors .= "Username is missing.\r\n";
    }
    if (strlen($strPassword) == 0) {
        $errors .= "No password given.\r\n";
    }

    if ($errors !== null) {
        //There was at least one error.
        //We show a message box with the errors
        $dialog = new GtkMessageDialog($wnd, Gtk::DIALOG_MODAL,
            Gtk::MESSAGE_ERROR, Gtk::BUTTONS_OK, $errors);
        $dialog->set_markup(
            "The following errors occured:\r\n"
```

```php
        . "<span foreground='red'>" . $errors . "</span>"
    );
    $dialog->run();
    $dialog->destroy();
} else {
    //No error. You would need to hide the dialog now
    //instead of destroying it (because when you destroy it,
    //Gtk::main_quit() gets called) and show the main window
    $wnd->destroy();
    }
}


//Create the login window
$wnd = new GtkWindow();
$wnd->set_title('Login');
//Close the main loop when the window is destroyed
$wnd->connect_simple('destroy', array('gtk', 'main_quit'));


//Set up all the widgets we need
$lblCredit   = new GtkLabel('Please provide your data');
//The second parameter says that the underscore should be parsed as underline
$lblUsername = new GtkLabel('_Username', true);
$lblPassword = new GtkLabel('_Password', true);
$txtUsername = new GtkEntry();
$txtPassword = new GtkEntry();
$btnLogin    = new GtkButton('_Login');
$btnCancel   = new GtkButton('_Cancel');


//Which widget should be activated when the
// mnemonic (Alt+U or Alt+P) is pressed?
$lblUsername->set_mnemonic_widget($txtUsername);
$lblPassword->set_mnemonic_widget($txtPassword);
//Hide the password
//$txtPassword->set_invisible_char('*');

//Destroy the window when the user clicks Cancel
$btnCancel->connect_simple('clicked', array($wnd, 'destroy'));
//Call the login function when the user clicks on Login
$btnLogin->connect_simple('clicked', 'login', $wnd, $txtUsername, $txtPassword);


//Lay out all the widgets in the table
```

```php
$tbl = new GtkTable(3, 2);
$tbl->attach($lblCredit, 0, 2, 0, 1);
$tbl->attach($lblUsername, 0, 1, 1, 2);
$tbl->attach($txtUsername, 1, 2, 1, 2);
$tbl->attach($lblPassword, 0, 1, 2, 3);
$tbl->attach($txtPassword, 1, 2, 2, 3);


//Add the buttons to a button box
$bbox = new GtkHButtonBox();
$bbox->set_layout(Gtk::BUTTONBOX_EDGE);
$bbox->add($btnCancel);
$bbox->add($btnLogin);


//Add the table and the button box to a vbox
$vbox = new GtkVBox();
$vbox->pack_start($tbl);
$vbox->pack_start($bbox);

//Add the vbox to the window
$wnd->add($vbox);
//Show all widgets
$wnd->show_all();
//Start the main loop
Gtk::main();
?>
```

http://gtk.php.net

12.2. Monolog v2

The new version of the most popular logging library is now only available for PHP 7.1+. It contains almost every framework integration like: Symfon, Laravel, Yii or any other framework which follows autoloading in PSR-3 format. Monolog sends your logs to files, sockets, inboxes, databases and various web services. The ability to attach many Handlers, Formatters and Processors gives endless features and customizations. An example below will show how to register 3 different fandlers: file based system, FirePHP and using database table.

```php
//pdoHandler.php
use Monolog\Logger;
use Monolog\Handler\AbstractProcessingHandler;

class PDOHandler extends AbstractProcessingHandler
{
    private $initialized = false;
    private $pdo;
    private $statement;

    public function __construct(PDO $pdo, $level = Logger::DEBUG, bool $bubble =
true)
    {
        $this->pdo = $pdo;
        parent::__construct($level, $bubble);
    }

    protected function write(array $record): void
    {
        if (!$this->initialized) {
            $this->initialize();
        }

        $this->statement->execute(array(
            'channel' => $record['channel'],
            'level' => $record['level'],
            'message' => $record['formatted'],
            'time' => $record['datetime']->format('U'),
        ));
    }

    private function initialize()
    {
        $this->pdo->exec(
            'CREATE TABLE IF NOT EXISTS monolog '
            .'(channel VARCHAR(255), level INTEGER, message LONGTEXT, time
INTEGER UNSIGNED)'
        );
        $this->statement = $this->pdo->prepare(
            'INSERT INTO monolog (channel, level, message, time) VALUES (:channel,
:level, :message, :time)'
        );

        $this->initialized = true;
```

```
        }
    }

//main.php
use Monolog\Logger;
use Monolog\Handler\StreamHandler;
use Monolog\Handler\FirePHPHandler;

// Create the logger
$logger = new Logger('my_logger');
// Now add some handlers
$logger->pushHandler(new StreamHandler(__DIR__.'/my_app.log',
Logger::DEBUG));
$logger->pushHandler(new FirePHPHandler());

//add DB handler
$logger->pushHandler(new PDOHandler(new PDO('sqlite:logs.sqlite')));

// You can now use your logger
$logger->info('My logger is now ready');
```

https://github.com/Seldaek/monolog

12.3. Carbon

Carbon is a simple PHP API extension for `DateTime` PHP package created by Brian Nesbit. It provides functionality of converting datetime into human readable formats, comparing two dates, easily dealing of timezones and macro available.

We can have some advanced usages of `DateTime` object in addition to built-in features in PHP 7.

```
$sunday = new Carbon('first sunday of 2019');
$monday = new Carbon('first monday of 2019');

echo implode(', ', Carbon::getWeekendDays());
// 6, 0
var_dump($sunday->isWeekend());
// bool(true)
var_dump($monday->isWeekend());
// bool(false)
```

```
$date1 = Carbon::createMidnightDate(2016, 1, 5);
$date2 = Carbon::createMidnightDate(2017, 3, 15);

echo $date1->diffInDays($date2);
 // 435
echo $date1->diffInWeekdays($date2);
 // 311
echo $date1->diffInWeekendDays($date2);
 // 124

echo $date1->diffInWeeks($date2);
 // 62
echo $date1->diffInMonths($date2);
 // 14
echo $date1->diffInYears($date2);
 // 1
```

Carbon could be also used to display human readable formats, for instance on our blog or posted comments:

```
echo Carbon::now()->subDays(5)->diffForHumans();
// 5 days ago
echo Carbon::now()->diffForHumans(Carbon::now()->subYear());
// 1 year after

$dt = Carbon::createFromDate(2011, 8, 1);
echo $dt->diffForHumans($dt->copy()->addMonth());
// 1 month before

echo $dt->diffForHumans($dt->copy()->subMonth());
// 1 month after
echo Carbon::now()->addSeconds(5)->diffForHumans();
// 5 seconds from now

echo Carbon::now()->subDays(24)->diffForHumans();
// 3 weeks ago
echo Carbon::now()->subDays(24)->longAbsoluteDiffForHumans();
// 3 weeks

echo Carbon::parse('2019-08-03')->diffForHumans('2019-08-13');
// 1 week before
echo Carbon::parse('2000-01-01 00:50:32')->diffForHumans('@946684800');
// 50 minutes after
```

```
echo Carbon::create(2018, 2, 26, 4, 29, 43)-
>longRelativeDiffForHumans(Carbon::create(2016, 6, 21, 0, 0, 0), 6);
// 1 year 8 months 5 days 4 hours 29 minutes 43 seconds after
```

https://github.com/briannesbitt/Carbon

12.4. Koel

Koel is a simple web-based personal audio streaming service written in
Vue at the client side and Laravel on the server side. Targeting web
developers, Koel embraces some of the more modern web technologies –
flexbox, audio and drag-and-drop API to name a few – to do its job. Koel
doesn't handle uploading nor stream from Spotify. Instead, you upload
your songs into a readable directory on your server – preferably outside
of your web root dir – and configure Koel to scan and sync that location.
Koel recognizes audio extensions like: `.mp3`, `.ogg`, `.m4a` and `.flac`.

https://github.com/phanan/koel

12.5. Intervention Image

The Intervention Image library is also called "a phpThumb successor"
which handles image manipulations and translations. The class is written
to make PHP image manipulating easier and more expressive. No matter
if you want to create image thumbnails, watermarks or format large
image files, Intervention Image helps you to manage every task in an
easy way with as little lines of code as possible.

```
// open an image file
$img = Image::make('public/foo.jpg');

// resize image instance
$img->resize(320, 240);

// insert a watermark
$img->insert('public/watermark.png');
```

```
// save image in desired format
$img->save('public/bar.jpg');
```

https://github.com/Intervention/image

Index